50 SHADES
OF LIFE, LOVE, & LAUGHTER

Reflections on Gratitude,
Joy, Life's Oddities...
And a Few Complaints!

LARRY GRIMALDI

**50 Shade of Life, Love & Laughter: Reflections on Gratitude, Joy, life's Oddities…
And a Few Complaints!**
Copyright © 2020 Larry Grimaldi.

Produced and printed
by Stillwater River Publications.
All rights reserved. Written and produced in the
United States of America.
This book may not be reproduced
or sold in any form without
the expressed, written
permission of the author and publisher.
Visit our website at
www.StillwaterPress.com
for more information.
First Stillwater River Publications Edition
ISBN: 978-1-952521-30-0
2 3 4 5 6 7 8 9 10
Written by Larry Grimaldi
Published by Stillwater River Publications,
Pawtucket, RI, USA.

*The views and opinions expressed
in this book are solely those of the author
and do not necessarily reflect the views
and opinions of the publisher.*

DEDICATIONS

To Kathy:
Thanks for sharing more than 50 years
of Life, Love, and Laughter
And Everything in Between!

To Kate, Matt, and Ben:
Thanks for your love and support!

To Katharine ElanaLyn, Sophia Grace,
Nicholas Lawrence, and Benjamin Dale, Jr.:
May your days be filled with Life, Love, and Laughter.

TABLE OF CONTENTS

MUSINGS AND MEMORIES

INTRODUCTION

In retrospect, *Fifty Shades of Life, Love, and Laughter* began with a feature article I wrote for *Senior Digest* in 2000 describing the last reunion of my Crary Street neighborhood.

The lower end of Crary Street, where I lived in a tenement until I was about 13, sat at the end of Eddy Street, hard by the Rhode Island Hospital. In the very early 1960s, the first bulldozers razed most of the multi-family houses, jewelry manufacturing shops, small variety stores, a dusty playground, and more than a few bars to make way for the first stretches of Interstate Route 95. The project completely transformed the landscape, texture, and make-up of our little corner of South Providence, Rhode Island.

Until then, Crary Street was a vibrant enclave of mostly first and second generation Italians living in family clusters. Most of the men, like my father, labored in the costume jewelry factories that dominated the neighborhood. The women were mostly stay-at-home moms. Very often though, they did "homework" (jewelry assembly tasks long forgotten such as stringing, carding, or gluing pieces) at their kitchen tables. They were paid in "piece work," according to how many pieces of costume jewelry they had worked on.

That first phase of Route 95 construction obliterated the neighborhood, save for three houses (one of them was mine) and a corner tavern. Some 25 years later, the three remaining houses were demolished for the upgrade of Route 95 that runs in front of the sprawling Rhode Island Hospital complex.

Today, Crary Street is just a memory for those of us who lived, worked, went to school, worshipped, played, laughed, and cried there before moving on (and out). The ghosts of the neighborhood silently drift away a little more with each passing day. Thousands of people drive by the vacant lots and few remaining structures in the Crary Street blocks, oblivious to the history of what was once a thriving neighborhood.

After I retired from my position at the Department of Elderly Affairs in 2015, I wanted to keep writing. During my 30-year career exploring the issues of growing older, I wrote newspaper releases and columns, fact sheets, service guide manuals, radio and television scripts, etc. Now I wanted to break out of the bureacratic mold and write columns about people, places, and things, register my complaints, and offer my perspectives on subjects of my choosing. The editors of *PrimeTime* monthly magazine granted me generous space in the Lifestyle section of their publication to celebrate my literary liberation.

Fifty Shades of Life, Love, and Laughter contains many of these columns, and a few bonus essays. I hope that you enjoy reading them as much as I enjoyed writing them.

Larry Grimaldi

FAMILY TIES

WE'VE TRAVELED MANY ROADS TOGETHER

Published November 2016, in PrimeTime magazine.

T he history and culture of America is rich in references to roads traveled during the journeys of life. In Robert Frost's classic poem, "The Road Not Taken," the narrator reveals that choosing a less worn path shaped his future. So what did Yogi Berra mean when he advised, "When you come to the fork in the road, take it"?

Bob Hope and Bing Crosby made millions of people laugh with their Road to Rio, Bali, and Morocco, etc. movie series. Every four years (although it seems the next election cycle begins when a president is inaugurated) we have The Road to the White House. When we are faced with difficult decisions, we are said to be at the crossroads.

In the lower church of the Cathedral of Sts. Peter and Paul in Providence on November 7, 1970, my wife Kathy and I began a journey that has now lasted more than 46 years. I don't know if it's the road less traveled that Frost speaks of, but it certainly has been a most interesting journey.

Since we are a society ruled by statistics, algorithms, and computer models, let's run a few of the raw numbers. In 46 years of marriage we have lived in and retired the mortgages of two houses; worked at eight jobs; driven 18 different cars, raised three children, welcomed three grandchildren; attended parent-teacher conferences, dance recitals, concerts, sporting events and banquets, and awards ceremonies much too numerous to remember. In fact, some of these events are being lived again with grandchildren. But as with any summary that relies on numbers, the numbers are just the opening paragraph in a real life essay.

What began with a marriage proposal on a rickety covered bridge in Vermont has evolved into a life experience with all the elements of a trip through time. Contrary to the current social norms, we did not live together before we were married. So when Kathy and I married, there was a sense of excitement, anticipation, hope, and of course, some uncertainty about the future. I'm probably a marriage relationship dinosaur, but I think our road was better. There was room for mutual adjustment, growth, and new discoveries along the way. If I had to do it again, I would not change a thing.

We have met the physical, emotional, and financial challenges that four decades of marriage will inevitably bring to your doorstep head on. Our relationship has endured and flourished because we believed in facing these challenges together, working through our differences, having a strong spiritual foundation, supporting each other, allowing each other the independence to live a separate, equal, and parallel lives, possessing a mutual respect consideration for each other, and trying to reaffirm and grow our love in small ways each day. Of course, a sense of humor is invaluable.

We are now retired. We enjoy traveling together, playing a little golf, spending time with our grandchildren, pursuing our hobbies and interests, and planning new adventures. Each morning begins with a summary of the day's agenda and each evening there's a look back at day's events.

While it's hard to capture the texture and context of 46 years in a few words, there are some things that I am certain of. Kathy and I have a great appreciation for the joyous times we have spent with family and friends. The good times far outweigh the bad. We are grateful for their support during our life challenges. While we plan for the future, we live life with a Carpe Diem attitude.

As with any relationship, there is room for growth and improvement. Complacency is not an option. Kathy and I look forward to new adventures, whatever they may be. We hope to enhance our mutual love and respect for each other during the coming years. The road we took together may not have been the one less traveled, but it was it was our road and our journey.

A lesser known Barbra Streisand song is "Why Did I Choose You?" The song closes with this refrain, "If I had to choose again, I would still choose you." After 46 years, Kathy is still my choice.

NOTE: *On November 7 of this year (2020), we will celebrate our 50th wedding anniversary.*

GRANDPARENTS HAVE MORE FUN

Published April 2016, in PrimeTime magazine.

Whether you believe in God, Allah, Buddha, Mother Nature, Fate, The Great Spirit, The Great Pumpkin, or you are an agnostic or atheist, two universal truths were self-evident. One, raising children requires people who are young in age or young at heart. Two, grandparents have more fun than parents. Allow me to explain.

Being a good parent requires patience, endless energy, flexibility, resolve, constant vigilance, effective communications skills, determination, focus, and an acute awareness of current social trends. Being a good grandparent merely requires a sense of humor and a desire to enjoy every moment as it is happening.

As a parent of three children, my wife Kathy and I found ourselves immersed in a dizzying array of vocations. At different times, we were meal planners and chefs, foremen in charge of chores, teachers, disciplinarians, coaches, youth group leaders, transportation captains, spiritual advisors, event coordinators, loan officers, travel agents, advocates, storytellers, employment agents, and many other roles too numerous to remember. We were responsible for teaching life lessons of cooperation, compassion, honesty, hard work, effort, civility, acceptance, tolerance, patience (I was not to good at this one), and kindness.

When did we have time to work, socialize, and negotiate the challenges of a relationship that has now lasted more than 45 years? While we were not always right, we did our best. It was amazing how much smarter we became as our children grew older. Talking with family and friends whose children are now also grown, this appears to be a common phenomenon.

For most grandparents, their role carries much less responsibility and more opportunities to re-connect with the enthusiasm, innocence, and joy of youth. It's definitely more relaxing. As the grandparents of

Kailyn and Sophia, 12-year old twin granddaughters, and Nicholas, our six-year old grandson, we provide respite to busy and stressed out parents, serve as a link to our history, traditions, and culture, and maybe, create a little mischief once in a while (more on this later). The grandchildren are allowed to and stay up a little later while savoring ice cream sundaes while spending the night at our house, eat an extra cookie, or take some extra time to just sit and talk.

Although they are reminded to keep some of our joint adventures under wraps, occasionally the details of our escapades are unwittingly leaked to their disapproving parents. For example, for many years the children stayed with us on Saturdays while my daughter and son-in-law were at work. When each of the children reached approximately their third birthday, they became willing performers in a weekly ritual. After we made our bed, they used it as a trampoline. They were the circus act and I was the ring master and spotter. Unfortunately, our secret was revealed on day and I was reprimanded me for my actions. The circus tent folded, but my surreptitious smile at the rebuke is a fond memory.

We have shared countless hours at the beach, picking strawberries, going to the drive-in, reading books, visiting museums, playing cards or board games, bocce, croquet and whiffleball, followed by a backyard picnic or barbecue. Sometimes, we even invite their parents. While my house may have slightly more relaxed rules, we respect the boundaries set by their parents and temper our discipline so as not to impinge on parental rights.

Unlike when I was growing up, minor infractions are kept within the confines of our home. When I was a kid, the entire neighborhood was an unofficial "crime watch" organization. Neighbors and would delightfully report the slightest transgression to my parents. I vowed never to become a "rat" as a grandfather.

Like many grandparents, we go to the girls' softball games, buy many boxes of Girl Scout cookies (the girls claim that I'm their best customer) and support their numerous fundraising campaigns. Nicholas is our fledgling hockey star, so we drive to rinks across the state for his games. However, we pass on the 7:00 a.m. weekend games in Bur-rillville!

Today's parents face many more challenges in raising their children than our generation. They must monitor their Internet use, Facebook accounts, text messages, and other electronic media. They must pay close attention to their circle of friends and all those they interact with. Sadly, the freedom of movement that we enjoyed as children is a relic of a bygone era.

As kids, we would roam our neighborhood, ride our bikes, and play endless pick-up games of baseball and basketball in playgrounds and on courts around the city. During the summer, it was not unusual to leave our house in the morning and return for lunch; have dinner and go out again; and play until "the street lights come on."

Nobody worried about who we were with or where we were. We did not spend precious time away from school or chores playing video games or chained to our smart phones waiting for the next social update. We did not need adults to schedule our games or settle our disputes. Our lives were much simpler and our parents' job of child rearing was much less complex.

If my children become grandparents, I hope that they will revel in the experience as much as Kathy and I have. May they feel the joy of spending precious moments with their grandchildren. After all, like blondes, grandparents have more fun.

A LETTER TO KAILYN AND SOPHIA

Published June 2017, in *PrimeTime magazine*.

*M*y Dearest Granddaughters:
in a millisecond on the continuum of cosmic time, you have gone from climbing the first steps to kindergarten to descending those same steps as graduates of junior high school. During those nine years, there were school projects, concerts, father-daughter dances, cross-country races and soccer games, parent-teacher nights, countless reports and math problems, and many new friendships.

Your parents are proud of you; not only because of your academic accomplishments, but also because you have become compassionate and caring young ladies. You have brought great joy to your parents, your grandmother, and I. The memories we have created with you will last a lifetime.

In a few months, your world will become much larger. Your high school years will offer you exciting new opportunities to grow and explore your potential. You will also face challenges that will test your faith, confidence, and judgment. You will leave adolescence and become young women. But that's a letter for another time.

You are trading your small school for a much larger one. For a time, it will be a bit overwhelming and confusing. Don't let it concern you. Freshmen are amazingly adaptable and you will quickly make the transition to a new environment. Be prepared for more stringent academic standards, but keep in mind that true success is measured by the quality of effort. You will have many academic successes, and there will be moments times when you are dissatisfied with your progress. Keep on working. If you do your best, don't harbor disappointment. In other words, take pride in your achievements and learn from your less successful efforts.

You will be meeting students from more diverse backgrounds. Be open to learning about new cultures histories, and traditions. Your own life experience quilt will be richer for it. Stay in contact with your current school friends; but welcome new friends. Some of these friendships may last a lifetime.

Cultivate your spirit of adventure by getting involved in new academic, athletic and social pursuits. These four years of high school will pass very quickly and I encourage you to take advantage of every opportunity that this new chapter of your life will offer. While this new step in your academic life will no doubt keep you very busy, make sure to enjoy your social life. Savor each moment of joy and laughter.

As for the challenges outside the realm of academia, you will undoubtedly see and hear some things that will give rise to confusion, doubt, and even some anger. Do not be afraid to share your concerns with your parents, your grandmother and I, and your friends. Isolation does not solve problems. Decisions are easier when a variety of perspectives are heard and considered.

You will make mistakes. Don't be afraid of failure. The learning process often requires failure before success. Your basic senses of right and wrong, fairness, and compassion will guide you. Learn to listen to and appreciate honest criticism Sometimes you will follow your head. Sometimes you will follow your heart. You will learn which to follow based on the personal growth and genuine instincts. Honest motivation can never be questioned.

You can read many philosophies about living and learning. I'm sure you will discover many along this new journey, and maybe even invent some yourself. This observation by Roy T. Bennett brings them into sharper focus. *"Never stop dreaming. Never stop believing. Never give up. Never stop trying and never stop learning."*

Your grandmother and I look forward to sharing many more joyous and memorable moments with you during these next four years. This next step in your learning process will be exciting, stimulating, frustrating, challenging, and a lot of fun. Live it one day at a time.

Love,
Mampie

A BIRTHDAY GIFT
FOR KAILYN AND SOPHIA

Published June 2019, in PrimeTime magazine.

Dateline: **June 12, 2019:** Blink your eyes. That's the blur of 16 years passing since you first wrapped your tiny fingers around mine and the lifetime bond was formed. Happy birthday, Kailyn. Happy birthday, Sophia.

No doubt, you'll receive numerous presents and cards to mark your milestone birthday. In the past few months, I've tossed about countless ideas for my gift to you before coming to a heartfelt conclusion. I give you our shared memories. It's a treasure that holds immeasurable value for me and I hope that it brings you joy from time to time on your journey through a life filled with endless possibilities.

I'll begin with the first time Mammie and I were granted our first official Grandparents Babysitting Assignment. You came to the house strapped into your carrier seats and fully equipped with a set of "instructions." We were courteous enough to hold our laugher until your parents left. Then we pretty much ignored the list. However, I DO wish, however, that we had kept the list for historical reference.

As toddlers and for many years after, you spent every Saturday with us while your parents were working. As you grew a little older, you would cook breakfast, usually pancakes or French toast, with your grandmother. I was always relegated to clean-up. From the age of two, you were willing members of Mammie's June strawberry picking excursion and crew members in the ensuing jam preparation and shortcake baking festival. Most Saturdays, we went to parks or playgrounds. Sometimes just read together.

I can still see the photo of you in the local paper as 4-year olds with hair done up in matching spouts and decked out in too-large soccer uniforms. As with any rookie, you would disappear into the scrum of players surrounding the ball. When the ball suddenly popped out from the gaggle of fledging soccer stars, the entire group would move in unison to the next gathering point.

I was happy to join your father as an assistant coach when you began your instructional and minor league softball careers. I can still see you in those oversized jerseys and too-big hats that were perched sideways on your heads. I'm happy that you have continued playing softball in high school and commend you for trying new sports such as volleyball and indoor track. I look forward to our annual whiffle ball, hot wiener, and Del's Lemonade Day each year.

Although you have been willing to try new foods and test your limits with new experiences, I can recall times when you were not so brave. You were almost two when we had an Easter egg hunt in our back yard. Initially, you were reluctant to step off the stone patio and onto the grass. You had the same reaction later that year on a family vacation at Cape Hatteras National Seashore when you were skeptical about leaving the safety of the blanket to walk on the beach sand. I've also placed memories of family vacations to Disneyland and the Dominican Republic, among others, into the treasure chest.

You have been ballet dancers, musicians, Christmas pageant singers, and engineers of school historical and cultural projects. While we have attended most of these events, I must admit that sitting through 20 to 25 ballet recital acts until you performed your two or three numbers was a little trying. I always waited for unscripted moments when the very youngest dancers decided to hilariously ad-lib their routines, or even just leave the stage in the middle of their number. I recall dancing with you (sometimes both at once) at weddings, anniversaries, birthdays, and other family events.

From kindergarten through the sixth grade, I was the official Kailyn and Sophia "school bus." We spent much of that 10-minute ride talking, laughing, or joking. When you were younger we used to sing the alphabet on the way. Later, we spend that time yelling or singing the math times tables so that you would remember them. I'd like to think that I am partly responsible for your academic success, but that's more likely due to your love of reading, your intellectual curiosity, and a desire to be your personal best.

I am delighted that we have shared a love of music and many other areas of interest. Having co-authored a cookbook with you was a joyful experience. I remember the constant laughter as we developed the titles for each chapter and collaborated on the introductions for each section.

I have saved your hand-written, homemade birthday, Christmas, and Father's Day cards and thank you notes. They are safely tucked away with many of your drawings and miscellaneous "art works." It is one of my birthday wishes that you always maintain your deep sense of gratitude and appreciation. My memory treasure chest also contains recollections of our many conversations on a myriad of topics, shared laughter and celebration of your triumphs, and the mutual comfort shared in our disappointments and losses.

So I present this treasure chest of memories and thoughts to you as a gift for your 16th birthday. It is given to you with love and anticipation of adding many more of life's large and small moments to it over the years.

Happy birthday, Kailyn. Happy Birthday, Sophia.

Love,
Mampie

UNCLE MIKE
AND THE ZERO HOUR

Published September 2017, in PrimeTime magazine.

I n the late 1950s and early 1960s, my family spent many Sunday summer afternoons at Goddard Memorial State Park in Warwick. My father, mother, sister, and I were often joined by a contingent of aunts, uncles, and cousins. While I don't remember who was responsible for staking out the area for our outing, I do remember that the site had to have a lot of shade trees. There were not many trees in the inner city of our Providence tenement house and the cool breezes were a welcome relief for my father and uncles from their workdays in hot, humid mills and jewelry shops.

To call this weekly gathering a picnic would be misleading. In true Italian family tradition, we packed up our entire Sunday dinner (salad, pasta, chicken and potatoes, etc.) for the ride to Goddard Park. Metal green coolers held chilled seven-ounce bottles of Narragansett beer, soda, and summer fruits. Portable radios broadcast the familiar voice of Red Sox announcer Curt Gowdy describing the action for both ends of a double header. Sometime during the afternoon, one of the adults would walk the kids down to the beach for a swim.

These outdoor parties were filled with lively conversation (they, aunts, and uncles would switch to Italian if our parents didn't want us to understand what they were saying), laughter, and frequent debates about the Red Sox and Yankees. Since the Sox were not very good in those days, the ongoing discussion would always end up with the Ted Williams and Joe DiMaggio question. Who was the better player?

It all seems pretty idyllic, doesn't it? And it was, until that fateful Sunday about the middle of August each year. Every kid knew it was coming, but we were powerless to stop it…Uncle Mike's annual heralding of the upcoming school year.

I loved Uncle Mike. He was a happy person who joked often. He was the creator of the family's heirloom meatball recipe. For all his good

11

qualities, he had a particularly aggravating way of delivering his annual message. Uncle Mike would lean back, beer in hand, and announce, "Zero Hour is coming." We all knew what he was talking about.

Webster's dictionary describes Zero Hour as, "The time when a military operation is scheduled to begin." For a kid, Zero Hour was scheduled to invade and conquer our summer vacation right after Labor Day. From our juvenile perspective, September was a cruel month.

Uncle Mike's warning made us realize that our endless sandlot baseball season, played on a dusty neighborhood playground, would be ending soon. Our bike adventures would be cut short. Long hours in the sun would somehow become long days sitting in hard uncomfortable wooden chairs. We knew our freedom would be suddenly and unceremoniously yanked from us.

Uncle Mike's yearly proclamation of Zero Hour was verified by those annoying radio, television, and newspaper ads for "Back to School" sales. From the moment Uncle Mike declared that the school year was just around the corner, it seemed that the black cloud hovered over the last precious days of our summer vacation.

Today, I'm sure that today's schoolchildren feel even more harassed even by the early and constant barrage of "Back to School" ads and the constant online reminders. I feel badly for my grandchildren.

Many school systems now begin the academic year before Labor Day, so the summer recess could be even shorter than in my era. Uncle Mike would undoubtedly break out in a wide grin, despite the fact that he would have to move his dire warning of the impending school year up a week or so. Out of sympathy for my grandchildren, I have no desire to continue Uncle Mike's Zero Hour tradition. We will, however, continue to use his family recipe for meatballs!

PARENTING IN THE NEW AGE

Published December 2017, in *PrimeTime magazine*.

Having completing the job of raising our three children 20 years ago, my wife Kathy and I watch my daughter and her husband negotiate the minefields of modern day parenting. With some degree of objectivity, we see them working together to solve the mysteries of parenting twin teenage granddaughters and a younger grandson.

Witnessing this daily process unfold, we have reached three undeniable conclusions. One, we don't envy today's parents. Two, balancing a profession and family life is a formidable task. Three, maintaining constant vigilance in a world full of trap doors leading to dangerous roads for today's children is a necessity.

The most important challenge facing today's parents is the need to balance time spent on the job and time spent at home (and quite frankly with each other and their own social lives). Unlike my youth, today's economic realities have ushered in the era of the two-income family. The Bureau of Labor Statistics notes that in 61 percent of households raising children 18 and under, both spouses worked outside the home.

The term "quality time" may seem frayed and trite. However, time spent as a family eating dinner together when possible, playing games, going on family outings, or just talking is important for keeping communications lines open. Effective communications build trust. Solid trust is a crucial element when children are having problems, or when they are going through the inevitable transition periods. The bumps and bruises of the maturation process can be eased by two-way conversation.

Today's parents have to be experts at time management, organization, and scheduling. They become de facto traffic managers. A calendar with very large squares for writing the month's practices, games, rehearsals, recitals, music lessons, in addition to other school and social activities is a valuable backup to schedules stored in smart phones.

These notes mysteriously evaporate from "the cloud" now and then. Patience, flexibility, and grandparents who live close enough to help with transportation are also very helpful. A sense of humor is absolutely necessary.

In addition to teaching their children basic rules for personal safety, modern parents face an even bigger challenge that did not exist when I was growing up-the continuous threats posed by the cyber world.

We spent countless hours riding bikes, playing baseball, football, or basketball games at local playgrounds, or recreation centers. While we were aware of bullying, harassment, or the fear kidnapped, these threats did not cast a cloud over our activities. Today, parents must know who their kids are with and where they are at all times. In other words, they are full-time security guards.

Advanced computer technology, the Internet, smart phones, and social media are serious concerns for parents. They must keep up-to-date on these technologies because the cyber world is in inconstant and dizzying evolution. The cyber highways demand constant vigilance.

They must restrict access to certain sites. They must restrict access to certain people or groups they don't know. They must investigate contacts that they deem to be suspicious or potentially harmful. And they must continually review the activity on the child's phone. Cyber vigilance painstaking and time consuming as it is, but it may to be crucial to a child's safety and security.

While these electronic tools are often used for educational purposes such as homework or school projects, studies show that kids are spending time online texting, messaging, and using other electronic devices at alarmingly increasing rates. Controlling online time is tricky and parents will run into resistance, but these tasks are necessary elements to maintain balance in a child's life. Increased dependence on electronic gadgets inhibits interpersonal communication.

There is no authoritative manual for raising a child (setting aside the myriad of psycho babble, trendy, be-your-child's friend, helicopter, free-range fantasy tomes). Parents are always striving to achieve the right blend of discipline, while giving their children a chance to grow and learn (yes even from mistakes). Setting boundaries, while encouraging freedom of expression, creativity, and cultivating trust, are not easy jobs.

I would suggest that parents not strive for perfection, nor demand it from their children. Mistakes will are inevitable on both sides. When a child has given their best effort in school, on the field, or at any other endeavor, that effort is worthy of praise and encouragement. Sometimes scores or awards do not measure accomplishment.

Even choices that are made based on solid information, careful consideration, and good intentions may not turn out as planned. There is no doubt however, that life lessons are imbedded in every result, even bad ones. Parents cannot shield children from the outside world. Parents can only equip their children with the tools they need to face the challenges.

Yes, parenting in my era was much easier. I admire the efforts of dedicated parents, such as my daughter and son-in-law and countless others, to guide their children and prepare them for life in the real world (where you are not profusely lauded just for showing up). Their willingness to instill the values of self-reliance, personal responsibility, honesty, integrity, hard work, generosity, and compassion, seasoned with discipline, love, and a sense of humor reflect the proven basic tenets of parenting, regardless of the era.

I wish them, and all today's parents, well. The task may be exhausting, but the rewards are great!

THE APPETIZER

This essay was adapted from the introduction to Cooking With Mammie, a cookbook my wife Kathy and I published with our grandchildren to memorialize our Thursday night suppers.

My wife Kathy and are grandparents to 13 year-old twin granddaughters Katharine, also called Kailyn, Sophia, and Nicholas, their seven year-old brother. Grandparents link the history, culture, and traditions of past generations to the promises, hopes, and dreams of their grandchildren. Kathy has created a family legacy and tradition that envelopes all of these elements into a weekly tradition we call *Cooking With Mammie* (the name then two year-old Sophia gave to her grandmother).

On Thursdays, either Kathy or I pick up the kids after school and she takes the girls to the local grocery market to buy the food for a healthy evening meal, including (my personal favorite) desert. The fixings for the meal must cost less than $25. Under the watchful eye if their grandmother, the twins are responsible for the preparation and cooking of the meal. Nicholas is being indoctrinated into the tradition be getting out the pots and pans and setting the table. In fact, he has two of his own recipes in the book and is currently the designated meatball mixer and roller.

Main courses have ranged from pasta e fagioli (macaroni and bean soup) and other standard Italian staples to a fancier offering of chicken cordon bleu. The menu has included such delicacies as beef stew, four-bean salad, artichokes, meatloaf, broccoli with lemon, tomato and mozzarella caprese salad, tacos, baked cod, and something I invented called Saturday Evening Stew. In the interest of full disclosure, we ordered Chinese take-out one night.

Dinners are seasoned with lively conversations about school, music, softball, baseball, hockey (for Nicholas our budding center ice man), family events, and other subjects and issues that are important to the children. Jokes are liberally sprinkled into the chatter. In popular lingo, "It's quality time."

Our collective experiences lead us to the naming this anthology of personal recipes as *Cooking With Mammie."* Thus far, Saturday Evening Stew and Italian tuna fish are my only contributions to this culinary collection. We placed the chapter on deserts FIRST in our book. We decided that "Eat Desert First," despite mild disapproval from the children's parents, should be a goal that every diner should aspire to. One of the joys of being a grandparent is being able to create a little innocent mayhem every now and then that won't be revealed for many years!

Cooking With Mammie subtly teaches skills such as budgeting, shopping, meal planning and preparation, and teamwork. I doubt that Kailyn, Sophia, and Nicholas think of our Thursday evening dinners as a practical course in the culinary arts. Grandparents are amazingly clever and effective life coaches.

Cooking With Mammie is about creating memories. We are nurturing a lifelong relationship based on mutual experiences, text-free real conversations, humor, and, most of all, love. We all look forward to Thursdays. In our corner of this noise-filled world, we are spending joyous moments re-creating Sunday family dinners from a bygone and almost forgotten era. We are weaving a quilt of new traditions, helping our grandchildren understand the value of personal relationships, and keeping them connected to their cultural roots. Above all, it's just fun!

NOTE: Cooking With Mammie *is available online, or by e-mailing lvgrimaldi49@gmail.com.*

HAPPY THANKSGIVING – ITALIAN STYLE

Published November 2019, in *PrimeTime magazine*.

E very year when the calendar turns to November, I remember my favorite Thanksgiving story. I believe that warm and fuzzy holiday memories take on a mythical quality with the passage of time. If that's true, the tale I'm about to tell has all the elements of an Italian comedy.

Many years ago, my friend was invited to spend Thanksgiving with a large Italian family. Sitting down at the table at 12:00 p.m. sharp (as is the custom of most Italian holiday feats), he had no idea that he was about to be treated to a Thanksgiving meal fit for a king and his royal family (and most of the kingdom as well).

My friend came from a very small family. When he took his place the dinner table, he was automatically adopted into the family that included a large contingent of assorted relatives. He was also conferred the title of Honorary Uncle to the diners at the "Children's Table." Little did my friend realize that the dinner table was the "stage" where his immersion into Italian culture and cuisine would play out (complete with dialogue of raucous, lively conversation).

The meal began with antipasto. As he sampled the pickled peppers, artichoke hearts, olives, prosciutto and cheeses spread before him, he delighted to discover a new way to begin Thanksgiving dinner. It should be noted here that every family has its own version of antipasto. This explains the annual pilgrimages of tradition-bound family chefs returning to their roots and fighting the crowds at Italian specialty markets on Federal Hill to purchase the delicacies served at elaborate culinary celebrations (including Christmas Eve, the Feast of the Seven Fishes).

After the antipasto, soup was served. As he savored the chicken escarole soup, he began to wonder if he needed to cut down on the appetizers. After all, he didn't want to be stuffed at turkey time.

After the soup, the banqueters took a short rest to drink homemade wine. He eyed the Italian moonshine with some trepidation. But he didn't want to offend his hosts; so he raised his glass, joined in the Salute toast, and sipped. It didn't take long to realize that more wine would flow before dinner was over.

My friend was in for another surprise when the next course arrived. As piping hot platters of lasagna were set before him, he began to wonder if an Italian Thanksgiving included the American menu of "turkey and all the fixings." But the lasagna looked too tempting and the aroma was too enticing for him to pass up. Exhorted by the group's "Mangia" battle cry, he devoured the lasagna.

At long last, the turkey and traditional side dishes were served. As he was enjoying his dinner, (in much smaller portions than he was used to), my friend reminded himself to save room for dessert. The stage was set for another Thanksgiving revelation.

Pies were in shorter supply than he anticipated; but large serving dishes packed with an assortment of nuts, fruits, figs, dates, accompanied by a selection of Italian cookies and other baked treats was were new to his palate. There was also an assortment of after-dinner aperitifs such as anisette, sambucca, and amaretto (no Bailey's Irish Crème to be found) destined to lace the inevitable pot of espresso. The aperitifs are poured into the espresso as an Old World remedy for the over-taxed digestive tract.

After the feast had ended and the table was cleared, he realized that Thanksgiving dinner, played out against the constant hum of joyful conversation, had gone on for more than eight hours! My friend realized that he had enjoyed every moment; and he was particularly proud of his Honorary Uncle status.

Here's hoping that you enjoy your Thanksgiving feast in the company of family and friends. And if you're invited, don't miss the chance to celebrate Thanksgiving-Italian Style!

PEOPLE

RHODE ISLAND'S MUSIC MAN

Published June 2016, in PrimeTime magazine.

Browsing through DiMeglio's Music Store in Johnston is like strolling through a crowded bazaar in Marrakesh. You'll likely hear music lessons drifting from the small studio in the shop. You can examine the extensive stock of musical instruments including electric and acoustic guitars, drums, tubas, trumpets, clarinets, saxophones, violins, accordions, mandolins, a stringed instrument called a dulcimer, music books, and all types of equipment. You could marvel at the incredible artisanship and intricate detail of an antique box accordion handmade in Italy. Or, you can admire the other antique instruments, statues, and a framed poster of Bruce Springsteen. But the real treasure in DiMeglio's Music Store is its owner, 89 year-old Ed DiMeglio.

Ed was born on January 7, 1927 in the Cranston Street Armory district of Providence to an Italian immigrant father, John, and an American mother, Rafaella. Ed's father sold pianos for now-closed stores in downtown Providence such as the Outlet and Shepard's, and often played Italian favorites on the piano and mandolin.

In 1935, Ed's father opened a small music store at the corner of Westminster and Greene Streets in the city. Ed began taking accordion lessons and working in the store after school at age 8. He smiles as he recalls himself, his father, and his younger brother Lucio, who played the guitar, giving impromptu concerts for the customers. Lucio later switched to the bass fiddle. In 1951, the store was destroyed in fire. Ed's father re-opened the business at a location near the Cathedral of Saints Peter and Paul.

Ed remembers the store being open until 11:00 p.m. on Saturdays to repair instruments or supply equipment to musicians who were playing that night. Ed's father also sowed the seeds of his son's entrepreneurship. Every week, he would give Ed a few dollars to scour shops on South Main Street for antique musical instruments. Ed learned to recognize quality instruments. He would later put these skills to good use as an antique dealer.

One day, a musician walked into the store to buy an accordion. While he didn't have all the money he needed to buy an accordion, he struck a deal with Ed's father. Since the musician also worked in a poultry store, Ed showed up once a week to pick up a fresh chicken until the accordion was paid off.

One of Ed's fondest memories of his early years centers around an old tradition called serenading. The night before a wedding, Ed would accompany the groom to bride's home. While the girl sat in the window, Ed would play the accordion and the groom would sing. Some of the Romeos were not good crooners, so they would speak the song's lyrics.

Ed's life and future careers were nearly derailed as a teenager. He was born with a congenital heart defect and spent more than 40 days in Rhode Island Hospital battling a streptococcal virus that settled around his heart. A new miracle drug called penicillin saved his life. Ed quit high school and went to work in the music store, teaching the accordion and helping his father. Eventually, he earned his GED and took over the business.

Ed's eyes sparkle as he talks about meeting Dolores, his wife and "love of his life" for 66 years. Each day after closing the music store, Ed, his father, and his brother would walk home via Hoyle Square (where Central and Classical High Schools now stand). Ed met Dolores at the open air market in Hoyle Square and the romance began. They married, settled in Johnston, and raised a family of three children, Edmund, Dolores, and Tina Marie. The clan now includes six grandchildren and four great grandchildren.

In the early 1960s Ed formed an alliance with maestro Eugenio Feole to give music lessons at the store. Feole was hired on the advice of Ray Muffet, who owned Muffet's Music Store on Empire Street in Providence. Ed gave accordion lessons and Feole taught the saxophone, trumpet, and clarinet, and other band instruments. The school grew to 45 students and yearly concerts were held at the RI School of Design Auditorium. Add music promoter to Ed's resume.

Somewhere along the line, from 1955 to 1965, Ed found time to work as a cinematographer for Channel 12. Eventually, he was named as the station's chief cinematographer.

In 1967, Ed moved his music store to Putnam, Connecticut. At that time, Putnam was recognized as a Mecca for antique dealers. The lessons that Ed's father taught many years ago about buying quality antique instruments were about to pay dividends as he also opened an antique store and art gallery. By this time, Ed had also become very knowledgeable about jewelry, so antique jewelry was added to the store's inventory. In 2009, Ed was looking to move his music store closer to home. He relocated business to its current location in a former barber shop on Killingly Street in Johnston.

In addition to his careers in music as a store owner, teacher, and promoter, Ed has been an instructor and counselor to countless musicians. He has been a jeweler, cinematographer, antique dealer, art gallery owner, and a certified fire arms instructor. By the way, he was also an advisor to former Rhode Island Governor Christopher DelSesto.

With all that he has accomplished, Ed is typically humble when asked to summarize his amazing journey through life. "Given my health problems, I'm just happy that I'm still here," he declares. "Dolores is still the love of my life and my family gives me joy," he states. "I just want to be remembered as a good guy."

You can call Ed a Renaissance man or the Elder Statesman of Ocean State Melody. But he would be happy if you just call him Rhode Island's Music Man.

NOTE: Ed DeMeglio passed away in December 2016. It was my honor to tell the story of Rhode Island's Renaissance Man. The music legacy of five generations of the DeMeglio family lives on in a local music store that purchased much of the DeMeglio store inventory and offers music lessons to its former pupils.

EIGHT DECADES OF AUTOMOBILE SERVICE PASS INTO HISTORY

Published October 2016, in PrimeTime magazine.

One day in mid to late October, the lights will go out and the doors of the Sgambato Service Station in North Providence will be locked for the last time. The parking lot that served as an automotive triage where car problems were diagnosed before heading into the repair bays will be empty. Owners Billy Sgambato and his wife Sylvia are retiring and another valued neighborhood business will pass into history.

Billy's grandfather Giovanni started the business in the 1930's with a small store, gas station, and car repair garage on the same Woonasquatucket Avenue location where the current shop still stands. In 1948, the business moved into a brand new building. At the time, Billy notes, it was the largest car repair shop in the state.

In 1942, Sgambato Service became a Texaco franchise. They remained with the company for more than 40 years. Billy remembers the station handing out S & H green stamps with gas purchases. They got out of the gas business when meeting new tank regulations became a financial drain on the business.

In addition to pumping gas and repairing autos, Sgambato Service has been an official Rhode Island car inspection station, headquarters for a heavy truck towing business, classic car garage, and a snow removal contractor with more than 40 accounts. Billy laughs as he recalls hating late Saturday night and early Sunday morning snow storms because the four nearby churches would all want their parking lots cleared in time for services.

The Sgambato Service clan not only located its business on Woonasquatucket Avenue, but in a true reflection of the times, they lived in the neighborhood. Billy's Uncle Pat lived in the house next door to the garage. Billy lived next door with his father Ralph, mother, Ada, brother, Jack, and sisters Ada and Joan. Billy's uncle Frank lived across the street in a house on the same side of Woonasquatucket Avenue. Frank Sgambato served as a state senator for 32 years. He died at age 101 in 2011.

Sgambato Service is woven into the fabric of Billy's life. As a child he played in the open space behind the garage and did his homework at the shop. He recalls his mother taking the garage money to the bank every day in a paper bag. He remembers the gas lines of 1973 and being stuck in Vermont on a tow job during the Blizzard of 1978.

The 1973 gas shortage was a direct result of an oil embargo. Short supplies led to the legendary odd and even distribution system. Cars with even number plate numbers could buy gas on certain days. Cars carrying odd number plates could buy gas on other designated days. Stations flew red and green flags to signify whether or not they had gas to sell. Billy would stand at the end of the line in the street with a flag indicating that no more customers would be served that day.

Sgambato Service established a tradition of reliability and automotive expertise that is still the hallmark of its business more than 80 years after the doors opened. They have a reputation for providing honest service at fair prices. Sgambato Service also practiced an old neighborhood business tradition of keeping an "account" for trusted customers if they cannot pay their bill all at once. People would pay $10, $20 a week, or whatever they could afford, until their tab was paid. No doubt, this helped many families pay their household bills, or buy food that week.

Since announcing their retirement, many loyal customers have asked, "Where will I go now"? The business went up for sale. Billy and Sylvia would like new owners to keep it as a car repair shop. Time will tell.

The decision to retire did not come easy to them. But years of bending, lifting, turning, twisting, pulling, pushing, and crawling under cars have taken a physical toll on Billy. He has had one knee replaced and the other is bothering him. The rapidly changing technology of the automobile business also factored into the decision. And besides, after about 55 years of fixing cars, "It's just time," he declared.

They will miss the everyday contact with their customers. Billy notes that many children of parents whose cars he repaired years ago now use his shop. They are planning a two-week trip to Disney World in Orlando to visit with Billy's son. They have never really taken any significant vacation in more than 30 years, except for a four-day New Hampshire honeymoon. They will have more time to visit Billy's three grandchildren and Sylvia's two daughters and three grandchildren.

So what does the future hold for Billy and Sylvia? Billy realizes that retirement will be a big adjustment for him. He's going to take some time to relax and dercide what he wants to do next. Sylvia will continue to drive a school bus part-time and pursue her photography hobby. They will attend car shows and drive to cruise nights in one of their many classic autos, including a 1934 Ford Coupe, 1987 Chevrolet Monte Carlo, 1972 Chevy Chevelle, or 1979 Buick Riviera. They also collect Texaco, Coca Cola, and gas pump memorabilia. Sylvia collects Wizard of Oz memorabilia.

Billy looks back on his career with a measure of pride and a little regret. "We may have missed some family events because running this business required 12 or 13 hour work days," he observed. "But we worked hard, did well, and gave our customers honest service. It's time to live life."

If Billy and Sylvia live life with the same energy with which they ran Sgambato Service Station, it will be a life well lived.

WHITE OAK FARMS CULTIVATES FRESH PRODUCE AND A REVERENCE FOR HISTORY

Published October 2018, in PrimeTime magazine.

Walking past the zucchini patch to the apple and peach orchards at White Oak Farm, owner Roger Phillips, pauses to show you the ancient New England stone wall he has meticulously restored. The wall surrounds grave stones of the original land owners dating back to 1775. Roger realizes the past of his 79-acre farm in North Scituate is prologue to the next generation of the Phillips family legacy.

White Oak Farm dates back to 1909. Henry and Laura Phillips, Roger's grandparents, bought the property in 1937 to run as a dairy farm. When their son, Newell and his wife, Myra took over the farm in 1939 they turned it into an apple farm which eventually grew to over 3,200 trees.

Newell worked the orchard with his wife and sons Roger, Billy, and Kenny. They also cut and sold 100 to 200 cords of wood each year. Newell worked White Oaks while holding a full time job as a truck driver for the old Outlet Department store in Providence. In the 1980s, in addition to marketing the apples, the family opened the farm to the pick-your-own crowd for a few years. Newell died in 2002 and Myra passed away in 2016.

By 2004, White Oaks began a new chapter as a vegetable farm run by Roger and his wife Pat. The transformation was necessary because 25 to 30 year-old apple trees that had sustained the farm for so many years were producing less fruit. Today, Roger and his wife Pat are joined by their son Paul and his wife Jessica, in working White Oak. Grandchildren Shelby, Jackson, and Lily also pitch in. In total, five generations of the Phillips family have tended to the crops on the farm.

Roger and Pat are both retired and now manage the farm full-time. Roger was an auto shop supervisor for the Adult Correctional

Institution and Pat worked at Bank of America. Pat moved to rural North Scituate when she married Roger in 1972. Although she grew up in a house on busy, raucous Smith Street in Providence, she has learned to appreciate quiet country living.

White Oak Farm grows corn, cucumbers, eggplant (6 different kinds including a Sicilian variety-who knew?), summer squash, zucchini, green beans, gourds and pumpkins, tomatoes, and peppers. In addition to seven different kinds of apples, the Phillips crew grows blueberries, peaches, and strawberries.

You should treat yourself to a country ride, stop by White Oak farm, and enjoy the taste of fresh fruits and vegetables. On my visit to the farm in August, I bit into one of the peaches. The peach looked as round and perfect as an ad in a grocery store flyer; but the sweetness and flavor of the fruit far exceeded any photo! White Oak Farm crops make their way to your table through wholesalers, Dave's Market, or via Farmers' Markets in the center of Scituate, Goddard Memorial State Park in Warwick, and Fisherman's Memorial Park in Narragansett. Contact White Oak for dates and times.

Working a family has many rewards, but there are also challenges. A successful growing year depends on notoriously fickle New England weather, crop viruses and diseases, expenditures for supplies and maintaining farm equipment, buying starter plants for certain crops, warding off pests and foraging deer, frequently scaring off hungry bird flocks, and dealing with possums, raccoons, and other country wildlife.

I wondered why Roger still puts in the long hours and tackles the hard work that farming demands. His answers were simple and direct. "I love waking up early in the morning, walk out into the fresh air, and soak in the peace and quiet. I enjoy working with my family and I'm happy doing something I like."

When Roger began cleaning the old graveyard, he paused to read the weathered, fading epitaphs on tombstones of Stephen Colwell, his wife Martha, original property owners, their daughter Lillis, and son Stephen, Jr. It's important to Roger that he honors the pioneers of White Oak Farm, and I'm sure that somewhere the Cowells are smiling in approval.

White Oak Farm is located at 74 White Oak Lane in North Scituate. For information, call 486-9085 or 934-1576, or go to www.farm-freshri.org.

NOTE: *White Oak Farms is still in operation today.*

I KNOW YOUR FACE...
BUT *WHO* ARE YOU?

Published March 2018, in *PrimeTime magazine*.

I 'm not an actor, writer, producer, or director. Consequently, I have only a layman's knowledge of the credit hierarchy attached to entertainment protocol. The "star" billing is obvious, as are "also starring or co-starring" definitions. And as you scroll down a movie or television screen, or read your Playbill, you'll see the "with" notation. For the latter, I assign ensemble cast members to an "I know your face, but *WHO* you?" billing group.

In researching this column, I realized that many "character actors, also starring, or second bananas" have the ability to lift themselves, almost effortlessly, onto equal footing with the stars. Their impressive dramatic or comedic abilities transport us to a realm where their character, in that theatrical moment, is alive.

These remarkable and gifted actors create Art Carney's Norton to Jackie Gleason's Ralph Kramden in the Honeymooners. Tim Conway, Vickie Lawrence, and Harvey Korman were the comedy equals to Carol Burnett in the Carol Burnett Show (1967 to 1978). Many of the characters in the epic television series M*A*S*H* (1972 to 1983) achieved comparable artistic footing with star Alan Alda. Harry Morgan (Col. Potter), Loretta Swit (Maj. Margaret Houlihan), Mike Farrell (B. J. Hunnicutt), David Ogden Stiers (Maj. Charles Emerson Winchester), Gary Burghoff (Radar O'Reilly) Jamie Farr (Cpl. Maxwell Q. Klinger) and William Christopher (Father Mulcahey) were principle ingredients in the comedy/drama M*A*S*H* mix. Honorable Mentions go to Edgar Winter who portrayed psychotic CIA agent Col. Flagg and Allan Arbus, who was featured as an on-the-front line psychiatrist Dr. Sydney Freedman in periodic episodes. Bob Hope and Bing Crosby were equal partners in the "Road To" comedy movies.

Some co-stars are permanently imbedded into our entertainment memory vaults. Don Knotts (Barney Fife, the Andy Griffin Show), Jay

Silverheels (Tonto, The Lone Ranger), Amanda Blake (Miss Kitty, Gunsmoke), Agnes Morehead (Bewitched), Pernell Roberts (Adam), Dan Blocker ("Hoss"), and Michael Landon (Little Joe) were most recognizable as the sons of Lorne Greene (Ben Cartwright, Bonanza). You can include Abe Vigoda (Fish, Barney Miller and Tessio, The Godfather) in this casting group.

Some stars and co-stars were not even human. Flipper, Lassie, and Rin Tin Tin hold a special place in the animal "actor's" Hall of Fame. Trusty steeds Silver and Scout carried the Lone Ranger and Tonto over treacherous western terrain to capture the bad guys. Trigger and Buttermilk casually loped along the trail as Roy Rogers and Dale Evans crooned their way through the Roy Rogers Show (1951 to 1957).

Now let's turn our attention to the "I Know Your Face, But *WHO* Are You?" thespian category. First and foremost on my list is Mary Wickes. Her career spanned more than 50 years in radio, television, the stage, and movies. Wickes may be best recognized today as the ousted choir director Sister Mary Lazarus to Whoopee Goldberg's Sister Mary Clarence in the 1992 film Sister Act. But in her acting lifetime, she appeared in more than 25 movies, including The Man Who Came to Dinner with Bette Davis and Anne Sheridan in 1942. Wickes starred with Henry Fonda in the 1934 Broadway production of The Farmer Takes a Wife. She made guest appearances on television's Love Boat, Highway to Heaven, and Trapper John, M.D. programs. Wickes also co-starred with another "But *WHO* are You" actor Alice Pearce (more about Alice later) on the Dennis the Menace Show. In a bit of movie trivia, Wickes was the understudy to Margaret Hamilton as the Wicked Witch in the 1939 classic The Wizard of Oz!

You may picture Alex Karras as the horse-punching Mongo in the 1974 Mel Brooks classic comedy, Blazing Saddles. But Karras also appeared as a guest performer in M*A*S*H*, and was the featured actor in the Webster television series. Before he turned to acting, he was a four-time Pro Bowl defensive lineman for the Detroit Lions. He was suspended from the NFL in 1963, along with Green Bay Packer star Paul Hornung, for betting on football. Karras was reinstated in 1964.

33

Gale Gordon may best be remembered as the cantankerous, irascible, and ever helpless bank manager Mr. Mooney to Lucille Ball's Lucy Carmichael (Lucy Show, 1962 to 1968). However, Gordon accumulated an impressive list of television and movie credits during his career. He played Osgood Conklin, principle of Madison High School, in the 1956 film Our Miss Brooks. After the death of Joseph Kearns, who portrayed George Wilson in the Dennis the Menace television series (1959 to 1963), Gordon was cast as George's brother, John.

G.W. Bailey gave comedic life to the lazy, wise-cracking, Louisiana native Sgt. Luther Rizzo, a motor pool con artist in M*A*S*H*. Bailey also appeared in Police Academy movies as Captain Harris and as Lt. Louie Provenza in The Closer and Major Crimes television police dramas.

In my opinion, no actor managed to contort their face into a more bewildered, astonished, or pained pose than Alice Pearce. She played Agnes Kravitz on the Bewitched television series (1964 to 1972), starring Elizabeth Montgomery. Every week, snooping Agnes would peek into the Stevens' house and witness assorted acts of sorcery performed by Samantha, the witch-turned-into-sometimes-mortal-housewife in Bewitched, or another member of her other worldly clan. Of course, when she reported these events to her husband Abner, played by actor George Tobias, the magic was gone and Alice was questioned about her apparent "hallucinations." It was a treat to watch her magical mastery of physical comedy.

That's my list. When your next "I know Your Face, But *WHO* Are You?" moment comes, go directly to the Internet and solve the mystery before you induce a self-inflicted headache. Then, start your own list of favorites.

RHODE ISLAND PIRATE THOMAS TEW HOLDS AN IMPORTANT PLACE IN BUCCANEER HISTORY

Published April 2018, in PrimeTime magazine.

A recent stroll on a Key West pier re-energized my fascination with a chapter of nautical history labeled The Golden Age of Piracy, covering roughly the 1650s to the 1730s. Famous sea raiders William (Captain) Kidd, Sir Francis Drake, Jack Rackham (Calico Jack), Ann Bonny, Bartholomew (Black Bart) Roberts, Capt. Henry Morgan (of spiced rum fame) and others terrorized the coasts of Africa, Asia, Europe, the Caribbean, and eastern United States sea ports. Jamaica's Port Royal was a favorite pirate enclave. Lesser known is Thomas Tew. But in many sea marauder anthologies he is listed as Rhode Island's pirate.

Pirates are main characters in many tall tales. Some could be true and others are very likely romanticized accounts of actual events. Edward Teach (Blackbeard) plundered his way from the West Indies to the east coast of the United States in his most active years of 1717 and 1718. Blackbeard cut a menacing figure. He went into battle with pistol belts strapped across his chest and ribbons tied in his beard festooned with slow burning fuses. He would ignite the fuses as the fight began. Blackbeard was killed in a battle with an English warship on November 22, 1718 off Ocracoke Island in North Carolina's Outer Banks. Legend claims that his severed head swam around his boat, Queen Anne's Revenge, several times, before being impaled on the ship's bow as a warning to other pirates.

Most pirates began their careers as privateers. They secured "letters of marque" from European rulers that granted them license to raid enemy ships. The commissioning nation received a percentage of any captured cargo. As European nations formed alliances through treaties and marriages, privateering was eventually banned. Many "freeboot-ers," (another name for pirates) decided to continue their adventurous life style and became sea going thieves.

Buccaneer imagery created in books and movies are largely fantasy. Pirates were more thieves than murderers; walking the plank was rare; they disliked taking prisoners; and very little treasure was buried. Considerably more treasure was lost to the sea bottom in battle, bad weather, or ships running aground. Freebooter crews were governed more by egalitarian principles than dictatorship. The crew elected a captain and a quartermaster, who distributed captured bounty in equal shares. The captain usually claimed a double share.

Ships were governed by a code of conduct. Some of the rules banned gambling; declared that lanterns and candles were to be extinguished by 8:00 p.m. Drinking after 8:00 p.m. was to be done on deck in the dark. And, curiously enough, the Sabbath was observed.

Pirates were creative thieves. Nags Head in North Carolina was named for the practice of hanging lanterns around the heads of horses running along the shoreline. This string of light created an illusion of safe harbor. Once their craft ran aground on the shallow water that that hid the treacherous shoals, the unsuspecting captain and crew became easy victims.

Against this backdrop, the pirating exploits of Thomas Tew come to life. Although his birthplace is often listed as somewhere in England, or Greensboro, North Carolina, or another site, it's clear that Tew lived in Newport with his wife and two daughters during 1694 and 1695. Perhaps he was attracted by Newport's reputation as a harbor to unload black market goods. Some accounts suggest that members of his family may have settled in Newport as early as 1640.

In later years, Newport would condemn pirating. In June of 1723, Ed Low and Charles Harris (REAL pirates of the Caribbean) began chasing a ship off Long Island. Unfortunately, their target was the 20-gun war ship HMS Greyhound. Low escaped. Harris was captured. On July 23, 1723, 26 crew members were hanged at Gravelly Point in Newport (in the vicinity of Goat Island).

History records two Tew voyages. In 1692, he received his first letter of marque from the Governor of Bermuda. He was supplied with the 8-gun sloop Amity and enlisted a 46-man crew. His commission was to destroy a French factory off the coast of West Africa. Tew had other ideas.

Shortly after leaving Bermuda, Tew gained the consent of the crew to turn to piracy and set what he believed to be a more lucrative course. In 1693, Amity reached the mouth of the Red Sea and ran down a large Arabian ship with a crew of 300. Despite his manpower advantage, the captain surrendered without offering much resistance. The captured treasure was a pirate's dream! It totaled approximately 100,000 English pounds of gold and silver, jewels, spices, and other booty. By some accounts, it's still considered to be the largest haul in pirate history, with some estimates placing the value at $350 million in today's currency. Even if the value is vastly overstated, it enhances the mythical quality of Tew's reputation. He is also reputed to be one of the founders of Libertatia, an unverified pirate colony around Madagascar.

In 1694, Tew secured his second letter of marque from Benjamin Fletcher, Governor of New York. It appears that he had originally sought a commission from the Governor of Boston, but was denied. History also suggests that he obtained a Rhode Island letter of marquee, paying 500 English pounds to John Cranston. Sound familiar?

In 1695, Tew joined fellow Rhode Island pirates Joseph Faro and Thomas Wake, and enlisted pirates William May and Richard Want to assemble a freebooter armada. They hoped to duplicate the spectacular success of Tew's first voyage. In September, the cohort was approached in the Red Sea's Mandab Strait by a 25-ship Moor convoy. The convoy slipped by the pirates during the night and the buccaneers gave chase. After subduing two ships, Amity overtook the third ship and attacked. During the battle Tew was shot, disemboweled, and was killed. His dispirited crew surrendered with little resistance. Oddly enough, the King of England enlisted Captain Robert Kidd in 1696 to hunt down and kill Tew. He didn't know he was already dead.

Tew has passed into pirate lore, but his legend still roams Newport. On your next visit to the City by the Sea, stop at Newport Distillery and sample one of the Thomas Tew Rums.

NOTE: *This column was dedicated to my grandson Nicholas, who shares my interest in pirates.*

WHERE EVERYBODY KNOWS YOUR NAME

Published July 2019, in *PrimeTime magazine*.

Tucked into the corner of Homewood Avenue and Smith Street in North Providence is a breakfast restaurant that revives a culture of bygone days when variety stores, A&P markets, and local taverns were nestled in neighborhood landscapes. If they could talk, each one of this restaurant's seats would tell a thousand stories and offer thousands more memories of loyal patrons and local characters. Welcome to Cal's Corner Restaurant, a place where everybody knows your name.

For owners husband and wife Richard and Gina Califano, Cal's has been a labor of love for 36 years. They opened the restaurant in 1983 on the site of the former Penny Dick's Liquor Store. The 1914 structure originally housed Dick's Grocery Store. Before acquiring the site at auction, Richard had previously worked as an executive chef at several area restaurants across the state, including the legendary Smith's on Atwells Avenue in Providence, and eateries on Cape Cod. Gina wanted to be a dance instructor, but she eventually gravitated to restaurant business to work with her husband.

Opening Cal's was a leap of faith for the-then engaged couple, who married in 1984. Richard's father had reservations about his son's venture, but those disappeared with the growing success of this North Providence landmark. Cal's has earned the designation of Best Breakfast Restaurant, as selected by the readers of *Rhode Island Monthly* magazine. On weekends, cars line Smith Street and Homewood Avenue, and spill over into the parking lot across from Cal's.

The restaurant has undergone several renovations over the years, but it has maintained true to its neighborhood roots. Old movie posters and sports photos cover the walls. In addition to standard breakfast fare, the menu offers selections as the Italian Stallion frittata (an oven basked omelet for non-Italians), and a phonetically spelled morning treat "sangweech," an egg sandwich served with bacon, ham, or sausage on toast, and English muffin, or a bagel. For Cal's customers, the comfort food is matched by the comfortable neighborhood vibe that drifts on the tantalizing aromas from the kitchen. The warm and friendly atmosphere of the restaurant makes you feel at home.

Cal and Gina know most of their customers by name and they normally order. Gina advises the countless regulars to call ahead if they want the change their "usual" orders. While Richard is cooking, he often keeps us a running conversation with his customers, most times through the open kitchen window. The back and forth kibitzing puts the "Corner" atmosphere in Cal's Corner!

Richard and Gina proudly point out that they are now serving a third generation of customers. The first generation brough their children to Cal's when it first opened. Those children are now grown and bring their children to Cal's and the tradition continues. "We try to keep our prices low enough so the entire family can enjoy breakfast and spending time together," Richard said. He noted that the restaurant is a required stop on the itinerary when people return home to North Providence for holidays or just for a visit with family and friends. "My customer are like my family," Richard said. "I love coking for them. This is where I want to be," he added.

Gina recognizes the value of building relationships with the customers and makes it a habit to talk to each one as they take their seats. She knows that friendly banter makes people feel comfortable and she encourages the wait staff to do the same. Gina also realizes they are an integral element in Cal's long-term success. "Some of our people have been with us for more than 10 or 15 years and are part of the Cal's family," she observed. "Over the years, we have received numerous cards and letters from their parents who thanked us for helping their children grow and mature," Gina stated with pride.

Richard and Gina also believe that it's important to be part of, and contribute to, their community. Photos of many Cal's Corner sponsored youth sports teams hang on the restaurant walls. They also are generous contributors to many charitable efforts in their community.

After more than four decades in the restaurant business, Richard and Gina are planning to retire "in a few years," they said. Getting up at 4:00 a.m. every day to stop by farmers' markets and wholesale food companies to buy fresh fruits, vegetables, and other menu staples, and then cooking and serving customers from 7:00 a.m. to 1:00 p.m. (except Mondays) makes for as long day and a longer week. Recently, they purchased a camper and took it for a spin to Florida. They want to set out on the open road and travel cross-country when they retire.

Looking back over 36 years, Richard says that the secret of Cal's success was rooted in a very simple business philosophy. "We valued our customers and our staff," he stated. "When we walk away, I can leave knowing that I had a ball doing what I loved to do. My customers and our workers were our family," he said. Gina echoes those same thoughts borrowing a phrase from a classic Christmas movie by declaring, "It's a wonderful life."

The next time you're looking for a great breakfast in a homey atmosphere, visit Cal's at 1538 Smith Street in North Providence. Gina will greet you at the door. Sit down, talk, eat, and enjoy.

In an age of cookie-cutter chain restaurants hulking in monolithic shopping emporiums and non-descript strip malls, Cal's is a reminder of the days when you went to the local restaurant and enjoyed a good meal and conversation with family and friends. Cal's is a place where everybody knows your name and they're always glad you came.

PLACES
NEAR AND FAR

OUR GREAT AMERICAN ROAD TRIP

Published as the introduction to Wandering Across America

Our 2015 Great America Road Trip began months before we packed the Subaru with supplies, maps, and downloaded travel apps and backed out of the driveway the morning of April 16. My wife Kathy had retired from Brown University in January of 2014 and I retired this January.

Nearing retirement, we had decided that the cross-country journey would be the perfect way to kick off a new chapter in our lives. We had listed places we would like to visit and tossed them into a metal box (in no particular order). That random collection of destinations gradually evolved into a tentative itinerary stretching as far south as Tombstone, Arizona, as far west as Las Vegas, Nevada to visit our son, and to our northernmost point in West Yellowstone, Montana. California and the Pacific Northwest were not included in the trip because we had visited these locations previously. In between, thousands of miles of new life experiences awaited us.

For the record, the 2015 Great American Road Trip took 32 days. We travelled 8,766 miles and drove through 32 states and Washington, D.C. We bought 268 gallons of gas, ranging in price from $2.08 in Alabama to $3.16 in Las Vegas. The countless moments of wonder at the diversity of our national landscape or its people were priceless; our memories will last a lifetime.

Our first brush with history was crossing the Edmund Pettus Bridge in Selma, Alabama. The drive over the bridge evoked ghostly images of Bloody Sunday on March 7, 1965. Civil rights activists, lead by Martin Luther King, Ralph Abernathy, and Georgia Congressman John Lewis, began a march from Selma to Montgomery, Alabama to focus on voting and other rights. They were stopped at the bridge and attacked by police. Bloody Sunday became the seminal moment in the civil rights movement in the tumultuous 1960s.

New Orleans is dazzling festival of sights, sounds, and tastes. We had been to New Orleans before, but stops at Café Du Monde,

Brennan's, and Pat O'Brien's, were on the culinary encore list. We also enjoyed an elegant dinner at Commanders Palace. We sampled the spicy delights of gumbo, shrimp, and jambalaya, but we passed on the gator-on-a-stick at the French Market Place. On Bourbon Street, you can take 10 steps in any direction and become enveloped by jazz, blues, or zydeco. While we were listening to music and sipping a hurricane, it was time to engage in our favorite New Orleans pastime-people watching. Few other famous addresses offer such an eclectic array of characters.

New Mexico provided a few unexpected surprises. A visit to the UFO Museum in Roswell raised more questions than answers. Did aliens really crash in Roswell? Was there a government cover-up? Standing on the remnants of the old Santa Fe Trail, you could almost hear the rumble of covered wagons as they rolled over seemingly endless, foreboding hills and plains of the western frontier.

On the two-lane road leading to the Four Corners Monument, we passed through a small town named Shiprock (a curious designation for a desert community). Just outside the town, mammoth rock towers sprung sharply from the canyon floor. The towers resembled massive stone cathedrals stretching hundreds of feet into the sky.

In Tombstone, Arizona, the clatter of boots on the wooden walkways draws you back to 1881 when the Earps, Doc Holliday, and the Cowboy gang (perhaps the first organized crime group in America) sealed their place in legend and lore at the OK Corral. On a walking tour of the infamous Boot Hill Cemetery, we paused the graves of the outlaw Clanton and McLaury families. We chuckled at the gallows humor of one grave marker that proclaimed, "Here lies Lester Moore. Four slugs from a 44. No Les, no more."

At Zion National Park in Utah, a tram ushered us up, down, through, and around twisted roads carved into stunning skyscraping rock formations nestled into the prehistoric landscape. The muted reds, purples, browns and other colors painted natural portraits at every turn, each one unique in size, shape and shade.

In Yellowstone National Park, we watched herds of bison and elk amble over grasslands or lounge by their favorite watering hole. The next stop at a collection of small, steamy geysers prepared us for the natural drama of an Old Faithful eruption.

Standing on the hilltop at the Little Big Horn Battlefield National Memorial in South Dakota, echoes of charging Native Americans and the clatter of gun fire from the encircled U.S.7th cavalry seemed to float on the breeze.

In Dyersville, Iowa, our highway detour led us to the Field of Dreams movie site where the corn fields, farm house, barn and the baseball diamond remain frozen in Hollywood time. In the afternoon, volunteers dressed in 1919 White Sox uniforms pitched to visitors who want to create their own baseball dream.

Looking back on our 2015 Great American Road Trip, many vivid images are permanently imprinted in my memory.

-Desert canyon floors hosting bursts of dusty red, yellow and purple flowers.

-The whispers of history at sites such as the Alamo.

-Tumble weeds flying across the plains fleeing from an oncoming thunderstorm.

-Oil fields where working rigs mimicked toy plastic ducks dipping their beaks into water glasses.

-The spectacular beauty of a rainbow arched over the snow-capped Grand Tetons.

-The bohemian feel of Taos.

-Mountains, caverns, and treacherous roads hewn into the landscape by time, erosion, and the cacophony of jackhammers.

-The intimidating isolation you feel travelling roads framed by endless miles of flat prairies merging with distant horizons.

-The juxtaposition of modern highways with nostalgic Route 66 in towns like Globe, Arizona.

The Great American Road Trip should be at the top of any retirement "to do" list. You can clean the closets, paint the living room, or re-organize the garage some other time. America awaits.

NOTE: *A complete chronicle of our Great American Road Trip was published our book, Wandering Across America. Copies are available online, or by emailing lvgrimaldi49@gmail.com.*

IT WAS MUCH MORE DIFFICULT THAN I THOUGHT

Published May 2017, in *PrimeTime magazine*.

I thought writing a book would be easy. After all, I had spent more than 30 years writing news releases and columns, booklets, brochures, television and radio scripts, and everything in between. I even had my wife Kathy as co-author and collaborator. Surprisingly, it was much more difficult than I thought.

Let's back up a bit. When Kathy and I embarked on a cross-country drive in 2015, we had already decided to write a travel book about our trip. The book would chronicle our month long journey and rekindle our memories for many years to come. The book could also serve as a guide to retirees looking to begin a new chapter in their lives with an adventure defined by their interests.

Wandering Across America was based on Kathy's travel blogs and my notes in a daily journal. It wasn't too long before we discovered that writing and editing a book, finding a publisher, and marketing your product can be simultaneously daunting and exhilarating. While we had no illusions about selling hundreds of books or landing on a best seller list, we hoped to sell at least a few....outside of hawking *Wandering Across America* to family and friends.

The first step was to combine Kathy's blogs with my journal entries. This proved to be a challenging task. We tried to eliminate repetitive observations while preserving the tone and fabric of the narrative. Kathy and I had different creative perspectives. After many discussions, readings and re-readings, the original manuscript was completed.

Next, we needed to find a publisher who would guide us through the editing, design, and printing procedures for *Wandering Across America*. Since we are not named Ernest Hemmingway or Charlotte Bronte, we realized that self-publishing was our best option. We evaluated two proposals and settled on Stillwater River Publications in Pawtucket. The Stillwater proposal clearly spelled out their services and our responsibilities. Our partnership with Stillwater made sense because our investment would be modest and we could work with a local company. Stillwater not only patiently guided their neophyte authors through the process, but they also offered invaluable advice as to the size of the book, cover designs, formatting and presentation.

After an initial review of the manuscript, Stillwater developed the concepts and offered a creative vision for *Wandering Across America*. Their first impressions proved to be right on target. Despite our best efforts to avoid repetition, it was obvious that the manuscript needed more literary pruning. In some chapters, the narrative jumped from one entry to another, confusing the timelines. It was back to the editing desk.

After the second editing, the next step was to choose cover designs and select the photos for the book. Stillwater had sketched out five possible covers. Kathy and I mixed and matched their design ideas to assemble the front and back covers and we settled on eight and one half by 11 inch format. In the larger format, our 35 color photos would add graphic content to the narrative. We were not going to print *Wandering Across America* in color. But we quickly realized that black and white photos would not enhance the color contrasts and textures captured in the photographs.

Assembling the photo collection posed the next challenge. The myriad of pictures were preserved on phones, tablets, and cameras. Kathy's phone was broken beyond repair and her camera had jammed in mid-trip. Somehow, despite our limited technical expertise, we put together the portfolio and shipped the revised manuscript and pictures to the publishers.

Stillwater used the edited text and photos to create rough copy of the book and return it to us for review. It was exciting to catch the first glimpse of what was to become *Wandering Across America*.

After some technical change and minor edits, it was back to the publishers and await the first proof. Approximately 10 days later, we received the much anticipated proof. The suspense was building.

After some last minute changes and two proofs later, we signed off and *Wandering Across America* was off to the printer. On December

16, a shipment of books arrived at our house. Kathy and I were published authors! Notice of the book's release was posted online and on Stillwater's web site. I have to admit that it was gratifying to see the book being displayed for the entire world to see. There is a funny postscript to this tale. In February, our first royalty check arrived for the princely sum of $5.61. The report and a photocopy of the check have been framed and hang proudly and prominently in my den.

Publishing *Wandering Across America* was a great experience for Kathy and I. The metamorphosis from concept to completion was a learning experience. The many hours of discussion and coordination were tedious and frustrating at times. It WAS more difficult than I thought it would be, but it was worth the effort.

As a side note, the book contains an amusing irony. Although I made my living as a writer, most of the narrative in the book was penned by Kathy. The editors at Stillwater praised her ability to tell a story. Who knew?

Our next collaboration is already underway. We are working on a family cookbook with our 13-year old granddaughters Kailyn and Sophia. Stay tuned.

AN AMERICAN (AND THREE OTHER TRAVELERS) IN PARIS

Published May 2017, in *PrimeTime magazine.*

I don't like the term "bucket list." It's impersonal and has no emotional value. So when somebody asks about last month's 14-day adventure in Paris and the French countryside with my wife Kathy and our frequent travel companions, Arlene and Louie. I tell them that I was fortunate to live another dream-not cross an item off a laundry list. Dreams are woven from human emotion and a desire to expand our horizons. Travel is one of our retirement dreams.

After returning home and catching up on chores, mail, e-mails, children and grandchildren, bills, and sleep, I decided that the best way to remember the sights, sounds, and flavors of our French excursion would be to chronicle our impressions of the journey.

Paris is indeed the City of Light. In the evening, the Eiffel Tower is illuminated. Every hour on the hour ushers in a dance of sparkling lights in a dazzling dash up and down the structure. It is particularly delightful to watch the display on a river cruise along the River Seine. The Arc de Triomphe towers over the wide, elegant, tree lined Champs Elysees. The avenue of expensive shops and crowded sidewalk cafes host visitors and smartly dressed Parisians of many races, colors, and ethnic backgrounds. The harmony on this legendary boulevard stands in sharp contrast to our current national upheaval.

As you walk through the massive, ancient Notre Dame Cathedral, you are enveloped in an aura of peace and serenity. The multiple museums housed in the sprawling Louvre are a feast for those who appreciate the genius of the artists, painters, and sculptors of different millennia. These masters could somehow magically translate the majesty of art in their mind's eye to a canvas or block of stone.

Any trip to Paris should include a visit to The Palace at Versailles and its magnificent gardens. The priceless artwork, intricate tapestries, well-preserved rooms and furnishings, and the Hall of Mirrors bring to life the opulent lifestyles of such historical luminaries such as King Louis XVI and Marie Antoinette. Watching a performance at the Moulin Rouge you realize that the historical cabaret is the model for the gaudy extravaganzas of lights, music, and elaborate costumes in any standard Las Vegas show.

As an aside, we experienced none of the widely deceptive rumors that the French are rude and haughty. At every restaurant, café, and shop we were politely and cheerily greeted and assisted.

A short stroll through the narrow streets of Nice lead you to its expansive central plaza. If you walk just a little more, you will find yourself on the long promenade that parallels the shores of the French Rivera. The elegant hotels (some with nightly rates of more than 25,000 Euros) evoke memories of the resort's grand past and its glittering present a playground for the rich and famous. The renowned Cote D'Azur lives up to its name by exhibiting an amazing array of blue tints in the beach's waters.

One day of travel featured a contrast of venues that began in the medieval town of Carcassonne, a visit to the contemplative and holy shrines of Lourdes, the Grotto of Bernadette, and an overnight stay in the Atlantic Ocean town of Biarritz, another spa and recreational enclave for European millionaires.

The next day, we were driven to a small Basque French village where we boarded a vintage train and apex of the mountain. Even the delicious hot chocolate served as the end of the climb did nothing to calm my aversion (insert the word terror) to extreme heights.

During the tour, we spent a few hours walking the streets and narrow lanes of Monte Carlo. This tiny principality is the seat of the House of Grimaldi. While we arrive too late to tour the castle, I would like to return someday to visit my "cousins."

The most awe inspiring stop on the tour was time spent on the D-Day beaches at Normandy. It is almost impossible to visualize that 73,000 American soldiers scaled the perilous cliffs and stormed the well-obstacled and mined wide beachfront marking the beginning of the end of World War II. For more than cemetery.

A visit to the hallowed ground of the American cemetery should be required of every American as a reminder that freedom demands sacrifice, and these soldiers shared a common purpose-to preserve and protect the rights and freedoms guaranteed by the Constitution. They are witnesses to the principle that true patriotism rests in the heart and not merely in allegiance to physical symbols.

Our excursions lead us through the French countryside to the home and stunning gardens of Claude Monet in Giverny and the adopted home of Vincent Van Gogh in Arles. The stops in many small hamlets along the route offered much needed respite and a chance to explore quaint, picturesque hamlets that dotted our itinerary.

In one of these towns, we were treated to a typical evening meal on a small farm owned by our delightful host Beatrice. As was the case with many of our meals (save breakfast) we enjoyed sampling locally produced wines. We also look advantage of tastings in the Bordeaux and Loire valley regions.

The ancient castle of Chenonceau and its intricate landscaping and magnificent gardens gave us a glimpse of the life of French royalty who lived there. King Louis XIV (the Sun King) and his wife Catherine De Medici resided in this castle.

Our latest adventure not only fulfilled a dream, but also added to our trove of memories. At any time I choose, I can summon the images of France and savor the memories if this American in Paris, and his three travel companions.

OF MAGNETS AND MEMORIES...

Published November 2018, in PrimeTime magazine.

Like most hobbies, it started out small. As a kid, I collected baseball cards. For a nickel you could buy a pack of cards, scented with the unmistakable odor of a stale, stiff slab of bubble gum. If you were lucky, you might get a Mickey Mantle, Ted Williams, Stan Musial, or Willey Mays. More often than not, you would become the not-so-proud owner of Ted Lepcio, Don Buddin, or Jim Bouton (who was more famous for writing the tell-all baseball book Ball Four rather than his pitching). We traded cards or pitched them in winner-take-all, closest-to-the-wall matches. We also stuck them in our bicycle spooks to simulate the sound of a motorcycle. Nobody knows how many valuable vintage cards, thrown away by non-baseball fanatics' mothers, now rest at the bottom of the Johnston Landfill.

As an adult, my penchant for collecting re-surfaced in many different incarnations. I began collecting hockey pins. Those pins are stuck on a cork board in my basement. I still save ticket stubs in a wooden box from numerous concerts, games, and other events. Occasionally, I pull them out and relive the memories that they evoke. At one point, I amassed dozens of shot glasses. (I can host a party of 50, offer a toast, and many glasses would still be unused). I have collected match books, business cards, post cards, cocktail napkins, bar coasters, etc. My match book collection features relics from now destroyed Las Vegas landmarks such as the Dunes, Desert Inn, Frontier, Riviera, Westward Ho, Sands, Sahara Stardust, and Frontier Casinos.

Each item documents a small piece of my life, but my latest collection is a road map of travels and memories that clings to the front of my refrigerator-magnets. Why magnets? How did I get started? How many? What destinations do they reveal? Be patient, gentle reader. The answers are close at hand.

My magnet mania began with a very simple objective. I needed a place to keep appointments, the latest pictures of our infant granddaughters, family photos, letters and bills that needed to be mailed, and other reminders in an obvious place. I reasoned that trips to the refrigerator would serve as memory joggers. As I began to collect magnets from our travels, the souvenir garden seemed to grow exponentially and take on a life of its own.

How many? I didn't know the answer until our refrigerator of 30 years decided to retire abruptly. For the delivery of the new refrigerator, the magnets had to be removed. Finally, I had the answer to my grandchildren's' frequent question about the numbers of magnets clinging to the refrigerator. The inventory totaled of 127!

The mega magnet conglomeration is a chronicle of persons, places, things, and experiences, all arranged in a random, illogical, and unexplained order. Magnets had been purchased at stops made from Maine to Florida, Michigan to Texas, and from Massachusetts to California-34 states in all. Many were bought to create a magnetized landscape commemorating our 2015 cross-country road trip. Others mark journeys to England, France, Italy, Ireland, Monaco, and several Caribbean islands. Some of our favorites include an alien figure from the UFO Museum in Roswell, New Mexico, a hand crafted stone magnet from the Four Corners National Monument, a bobble head bison from Yellowstone National Park, smiling potatoes from Idaho, and the beach chair from Nice on the French Riviera.

Regardless of its origin, each magnet revives the memories of our vacations and adventures. From a logistical standpoint, the entire top freezer door is now covered by these souvenirs. By necessity, purchases have become smaller and the family travel log is now relegated to the bottom refrigerator door.

I don't know how long this hobby will last, how much I have invested, or how much I will invest. Someday, the entire collection might suffer the same ignominious demise as my baseball cards. But it's fun, inexpensive, rewarding and it reinvigorates memories of life stops along the way. Hobbies should be a reflection of a person's interests. My magnet treasure trove reflects my desire to travel, meet new people, and enjoy as much of life as I can.

A TRIP THROUGH HISTORY AND THE PANAMA CANAL

Published May 2019, in *PrimeTime* magazine.

A recent 10-day ocean cruise took us to the Panama Canal Zone. As we slowly made our way through the canal locks, I made a note to research the background of this 105-year water lane connecting two oceans. What I learned was fascinating.

The Panama Canal is a 400-year old epic saga that blends vision, history, engineering, technology, politics, finance, tragedy, and failure into a tale of ultimate triumph. As highly trained canal pilots (not ship captains) guide gigantic cruise vessels and immense cargo ships through the narrow locks, you realize that the 40-mile journey from the Caribbean Sea on the Atlantic side to the massive man-made Gatun Lake on the Pacific side is much more than an ordinary sea voyage. Canal passage, the system of three locks, where chambers are flooded to raise a ship up to an eventual height of 85 feet over sea level and power the ships through the Canal using a series of electric motors hidden in the canal walls, is an amazing experience. A crossing though the locks requires 52 million gallons of water drawn from Gatun Lake. Approximately 60 percent of the water is reused. Nature's rainwater replenishes the rest.

The Panama Canal saga begins in 1513 with the discovery of the Isthmus of Panama, a slender land bridge between the Atlantic and Pacific Oceans, by Spanish explorer Vasco Nunez de Balboa. His discovery began many futile attempts to find a water passage between the oceans. In 1534, Charles V of the Holy Roman Empire ordered a survey to determine if a water canal could be built connecting the two oceans. The survey concluded that the task was impossible and the canal concept lay dormant for more than 350 years. The prospect of eliminating more than 8,000 nautical miles from the Atlantic coast, around Cape Horn in Africa to get to the Pacific Ocean was still a distant dream.

In 1881, former French diplomat Ferdinand de Lesseps, who helped to develop the Suez Canal, formed a company and secured funding from the government of France to start digging the Panama Canal. Poor planning, rudimentary engineering principles (the company tried to build a canal without a lock system), and tropical diseases like malaria doomed the effort. De Lesseps eventually hired Gustave Eiffel to create a lock system, but the company went bankrupt in 1889 after France had invested $260 million in the project. Both de Lessups and Eiffel were charged and convicted of fraud and mismanagement by the French government in 1893. They were later exonerated. A few years later, another French company purchased the assets of the bankrupt de Lesseps venture to make an attempt at building the canal. Their efforts also failed.

The United States had expressed interest in building the Panama Canal in the 1880s; but their idea was to run the passage through Nicaragua. French engineer Phillippe-Jean Bunau-Varilla convinced the American government that the volcanic conditions in Nicaragua would endanger the stability of a canal, so the United States targeted Panama again.

In 1902, the United States Congress approved a purchase price of $10 million and an annual $250,000 payment to Panama for a 10-mile wide strip of acreage on the canal construction site. The treaty was negotiated by U.S. Secretary of State John Hay and Bunau-Varilla. The treaty also agreed to grant Panama its independence.

There was one minor hitch in the plan however. Panama was then part of Columbia and that country originally rejected the terms of the treaty. In a quiet attempt to support the Panamanian fight for independence, President Theodore Roosevelt dispatched U.S. war ships to the area as a show of intimidating power to Columbia (part of Roosevelt's "Walk softly and carry a big stick gun boat diplomacy") and Panama gained its independence in 1903. Canal construction began that same year, under the supervision of chief engineer John Findlay Wallace. The grand opening was celebrated on August 15, 1914. The United States spent $350 million to build the Panama Canal, but more than

25,000 people died during its construction, mostly due to malaria, yellow fever, and other tropical maladies.

There was one more political battle over the Canal that was yet to be fought. The original treaty called for the United States to control the Canal Zone in perpetuity. The mid-1960s saw Panamanians demonstrating to place their national flag in the Canal Zone and gain ownership of the waterway. Negotiations between the two nations began and culminated with the Torrojos-Carter Treaties in 1977. The treaties handed over the Canal to Panama's control on December 31, 1999. In 2007, expansion was undertaken to allow the canal to accommodate larger cruise ship and freight vessels.

Over the course of a year, an average of 14,000 ships pass through the Canal. The Panamanian government takes in about $2 billion each year in revenue from the waterway and $800 million is deposited directly into the nation's treasury.

In today's age of technology and engineering advances, it's amazing that the Panama Canal has retained its status as an effective ocean shipping route for more than 100 years. Technology has not diminished its economic viability. In fact, technology has enhanced its impact on global commerce.

The Panama Canal is a tribute to man's vision, creativity, and a stubborn will to succeed. If you get the chance, set sail on a Panama Canal cruise through history.

SEASONS

HALLOWTHANKSCHRISTMASNEWYEAR

Published December 2015, in PrimeTime magazine.

I n late September, I walked into a big box store to buy a bathroom plunger. What I saw froze me in my tracks. There before me was a chilling display of snow shovels, snow throwers, ice melt, windshield scrapers and washer fluid, and other winter battle gear. All that was missing was a fake storefront where Rhode Islanders could practice their sprints to the market for milk and bread when more than an inch of snow is forecast.

Hard by this display of wintery tools though, was an even more disturbing array of merchandise…Christmas trees, wreaths, ornaments, and other Yuletide decorations! Had I somehow missed all of those other holidays in between December 25? Was I in a time warp?

At that moment, I was reminded that times really had changed. We have now entered into an amorphous holiday season that begins on Labor Day and ends on January 1. It's called HallowThanksChristmasNewYear.

While Halloween marks the unofficial start of the holiday season (a kind of spring training for the days ahead), Thanksgiving kicks the holiday season into high gear. Remember Thanksgiving? Before it was merely day of rest before thundering herds stampeded through retail outlets in a feeding frenzy quite appropriately named Black Friday? Thanksgiving used to be a day spent with family and friends around a noisy dinner table with a feast that lasted for hours. Thanksgiving had its own place in American history, its own fall textures, and its own menu filled with savory foods and seasonal treats.

New Year's Day is notable only closing the holiday cycle and for making resolutions that are inevitably abandoned a week later. So, let's move on to Christmas.

My memories of the Christmas as a child, the Ghost of Christmas Past if you will, are still very vivid. After the customary pilgrimage through the Outlet department store, we would drive to the Farmer's

Market near the Providence Uniroyal plant on Valley Street to pick out our Christmas tree. Given my mother's superior negotiating skills, I can't remember ever paying more than seven dollars. The tree was set up and decorated in the living room. In an early version of energy conservation, the living room was normally closed off during the winter to conserve heat. Sliding open those hidden wooden doors for a few weeks was an annual ritual.

Of course, there was the time-honored Italian tradition knows as the Feast of the Seven Fishes held on Christmas Eve. As delicious as Thanksgiving dinner was, La Vigilia was the gastronomic high point of the year. Much to delight and despite her Irish and French roots, Kathy has adopted the La Vigilia tradition,. The only caveat is that I have to handle the preparation of the eels!

The Ghost of Christmas Past also draws out the memories of arduous 1:00 a.m. sessions spent assembling toys. I am mechanically challenged and unable to comprehend the "insert flap A into flap B and fold into flap C" instructions. These sessions were often filled with tension and aggravation that was sometimes expressed by a distinctly un-Yuletidelike vocabulary.

The Ghost of Christmas Present bears the precious gift of time spent with our children and grandchildren. Our sons Matt and Ben arrive home for Christmas from Las Vegas and New York City. Seeing the boys, my daughter Kate and her husband Ray, our 12-year old granddaughters Kailyn and Sophia, and five-year old Nicholas together for a few days is the holiday moment is our favorite holiday present. As a bonus, we are no longer are awakened at 6:00 a.m. (after a toy assembly session that ended only a few hours before) to see what treasures are under the tree. Thankfully, that tradition now takes place at my daughter's house!

With any luck, the Ghost of Christmas Future will bring with it more joyous moments with our families and friends. The moral of my Christmas Carol is simple. Cross HALLOWTHANKSCHRISTMASNEWYEAR off your calendar and take the time to celebrate each holiday for its uniqueness.

With proper apologies to Charles Dickens, the Ghost of Christmas Past is a reminder of quieter times when Christmas was a not a commercial venture and public displays were not lightning rods for faith-based controversies. The Ghost of Christmas Future holds the promise of creating memories that connect the culture and traditions of the past to the hope of days to come.

Most importantly, The Ghost of Christmas Present reminds us to savor each day, live with joy in the now, and tell our family and friends how much they mean to us. As Clement C. Moore proclaimed, "Happy Christmas to all, and to all a good night."

RETURNING TO FLORIDA AS A SNOWBIRD

Published January 2016, in PrimeTime magazine.

I am not Nostradamus and don't own a crystal ball, I can predict some 2016 events with absolute certainty.

My beloved New York Football Giants, with their Swiss cheese defense, will not win the 2016 Super Bowl. Unless the New York Yankees transform their roster from a collection of Social Security beneficiaries to a team populated by players age 28 and under, they will not win the World Series. No matter how many rounds of golf I play, my scores will not suddenly dip from an average of 100 to 72. Neither carnival barker Donald Trump, nor avowed Socialist Bernie Sanders, will be elected president of the United States. And my wife Kathy and I will officially become snowbirds. Between Martin Luther King Day and March 1, we will be temporary transplanted Floridians.

Our winter migration is the convergence of two unrelated, but very significant, circumstances. First, the icy images of last year's Siberian Winter still terrorize my memory bank. Secondly, my son Matthew recently purchased a vacation condo in Ft. Lauderdale. Motivated by either generosity or partial atonement for traditional teenage transgressions of many years ago (I prefer to think it's the former), he has offered us free lodging at the condo.

This impending seasonal immigration to South Florida prompts memories of the only the family vacation we ever took- Providence to Florida in October of 1960. My mother, father, sister Maryann piled into a mammoth Oldsmobile 88 owned by my aunt Mary and uncle Domenic for a two-week visit with their daughter in Miami, Florida.

Never having been anywhere farther than Albany, New York, the anticipation that surrounded this trip was incredible. In what seemed like a gift from the heavens, my sister and I got permission to leave school. While the conventional reasoning was that the trip would provide countless lessons in geography and history, I reveled in the secret joy of being paroled from Tyler School and the disciplinarians known as the Sisters of Mercy for two weeks!

The adventure was noteworthy for several reasons. In 1960, the construction of Interstate 95 had progressed as far as Richmond, Virginia. A large, yellow and black road sign and very tall wooden blockade proclaimed that this was the end of the modern highway. The rest of the journey would be traveled via the narrow roadway, framed by foreboding swamps, that meandered through the Carolinas and Georgia. The musty odor of drooping moss hanging from ancient trees still lingers in my memory bank. We passed by peanut fields and acres of growing cotton. Remnants of rundown empty ramshackle farm cabins still stood as silent witnesses to another era.

When we finally reached Miami and my cousin's house, I marveled at the tantalizing smell of a lemon tree growing in their back yard. On the short drive to Miami Beach, we passed the by the elegant Fountainbleu Hotel. Later, we walked the white sands of the beach and were treated to a circus of acrobatic flying fish in a nearby cove.

Since my aunt and uncle were staying in Florida a little longer, our journey home was booked by train from Miami to New York City. My love of train travel was born on this trip. While my memory wants to tab this train as the Gold Coast Railroad, research identified the caravan north as the Silver Star. The hypnotic rhythm of the cars clattering over the tracks made sleeping during the 1,500 overnight haul very easy.

After getting off the train in New York City, I got my first look at the world's most wondrous, and yes frightening, city. Skyscrapers rising though the clouds, yawning street canyons, and the deafening array of competing sounds dwarfed Boston. The whirlwind of sights and sounds was very intimidating to an 11-year old, and I was glad to board the New Haven train to Providence and home.

While the sense of adventure and anticipation may not be the same as it was 55 years ago, this year's Florida stay promises new status as a snow bird and a refuge from yet another Arctic winter predicted by the Farmer's Almanac. I suspect the Almanac is right because my backyard is littered by thousands of acorn crowns left by industrious squirrels. I can also take comfort in the knowledge that Interstate 95 now extends all the way to Miami!

NOTE: *It's apparent that my ability to predict election results is faulty. Donald Trump was elected President of the United States in November 2016.*

LAZY HAZY CRAZY DAYS OF PAST SUMMERS

Published July 2017, in *PrimeTime magazine*.

Sitting under the patio umbrella sipping an ice coffee is a great way to spend a July afternoon. Once in a while, a breeze comes up and carries with it the memories of summers past, summers as a kid growing up in South Providence.

My Crary Street neighborhood sat on the edge of Eddy Street, a stone's throw from the entrance to Rhode Island Hospital. The lower end of Crary Street was a mishmash of one-family houses, tenements and apartment buildings, bars, a gas station, a spa (convenience store in today's parlance), mattress warehouse, sandwich shops and restaurants, and numerous small and large costume jewelry factories. The rag man and the ice man would rumble occasionally through the neighborhood in horse drawn carts, as if to remind us of days gone by. There are no remnants of my neighborhood today. It was obliterated by the construction of Interstate Route 95 more than 50 years ago.

Across the street from the Samuels Dental Clinic on the grounds of Rhode Island Hospital campus sits a small triangular parking lot. Very few passers-by would realize that the lot stands as a silent reminder of what was our neighborhood playground. As kids, we spent countless hot, sticky summer hours in this recreational oasis, nestled in the inner city landscape. We played baseball, soared on the swings, competed in furious knock hockey games, or fashioned gimp jewelry in the small playground clubhouse. We were free to settle our disputes without adult intervention. Our diamond dream was to smash a baseball about 300 feet over the left field fence into the Atlantic Seaboard truck terminal across the street. No one ever did.

The daily summer routine was simple. After breakfast, you laced up your high-top Red Ball Jets sneakers (the one pair you got for the summer after a trip to the barber for the standard buzz hair cut) and set out for the playground. We played there until it was time to go home for lunch, then returned for the afternoon.

Our parents did not have to worry about where we were or who we were with. They had a secret weapon. If you got out of line, the "neighborhood watch" brigade of family and friends would promptly and gleefully report any transgressions, real or perceived, to your parents.

Sunday afternoons were spent enjoying family outings at Goddard State Park. A sizeable contingent of aunts, uncles and cousins gathered at a designated site. If you think the menu included hot dogs and hamburgers, you would be wrong. The entire standard Italian Sunday dinner menu of pasta and chicken, and other culinary staples were lugged the picnic site in huge pots. The metal cooler was filled was soda, fruit, salads, and seven-ounce "stubbies" of Narragansett Beer

After dinner, we walked to the beach or listened to Curt Gowdy call a Red Sox doubleheader on the transistor radio. If the wind was blowing in the right direction, you could catch a few scratchy sound waves of Yankee broadcasts.

When I was younger, many of our neighborhood families would pack up and move to small homes they owned at Conimicut Point in Warwick for the summer. On weekends, my father and my uncles would dig for quahogs in the cove. What wasn't pried open and eaten immediately would go into the spaghetti and clam feast that evening.

My grandfather owned a small beach shack at Conimicut Point, where we spent part of our summers. Although I was only five, I can vividly recall the awesome power of angry brown waves pounding the cove during Hurricane Carol in 1954. After we left the shack and headed for home, Carol swept the shack into the sea, leaving not one board, window, door, or stone in its wake.

Once a year, we were treated to an amusement park outing at Rocky Point in Warwick or Crescent Park in East Providence. The sights, sounds, and smells of the parks are still locked in my memory bank. When we take our grandchildren to the historic Looff Carousel at Crescent Park, or stroll the open spaces that where Rocky Point once stood, these images are replayed in my head.

I came to regard Labor Day with the same disdain as New Year's Day. Those dreaded holidays meant that school was right around the corner.

Each day, tens of thousands of commuters round the Thurber's Avenue curb on Route 95 and speed by the exits marked for Point Street and other South Providence buildings and offices. They don't know what I know. A vibrant neighborhood once stood on those vast acres of vacant land. A playground hosted countless baseball games and knock hockey matches. Driving by the old neighborhood on my way to somewhere else in downtown Providence, those lazy, hazy, crazy days of my childhood summers in South Providence come alive again.

JANUARY IS THE BRIDGE
FROM THE HOLIDAYS TO SPRING

Published January 2017, in *PrimeTime magazine.*

So here we are in January, the most curious month in the calendar. The holidays are over and the reality of winter is about to set in. Although the observances of Martin Luther King Day in January and Presidents Day in February will offer a break in the winter drought of holidays, some people may not have another day off until Memorial Day in May.

After New Year's Day, January becomes the orphan of holidays. February has Valentine's Day and March has St. Patrick's Day. Even April has the income tax day filing deadline, obviously not celebrated, but nonetheless a well noted day on the calendar. If you scan the calendar, you will note that virtually other month has its own significant holiday.

So what shall we make of January?

The word January is based on the Latin term Janarius in the Roman calendar. The month is named for Janus, the god of beginnings and endings. When you think about it, January bridges the old year to the new. We reflect on the past and make plans for the future. The month serves as a preparation for February, famous (or infamous if you prefer) for its horrible winter weather in spite of its short duration. Remember the Blizzard of 1978?

During January, we try to keep all those resolutions we made for the new year. Even if we don't succeed for the entire year, the effort is made and hope remains that we will still make good on those promises we made to ourselves.

For school children, January puts them back into the classroom after the long Christmas break. While some students can anticipate a week off from school in February, others may have to wait until spring for a break from their studies. Most of all, we can remind ourselves in January that the next change of the seasons will usher in spring!

January is not totally without merit. As a youngster, I can remember multiple newspaper and broadcast ads for those January white sales? Do they still have those? For the avid and devoted bargain hunters, January is a festival of clearance sales. They can stock up on supplies for next Christmas or get an early start on their 2017 shopping (much more preferable than Black Friday, Cyber Monday, etc.). If you are really ambitious, you can start planning your summer vacation.

January may give winter sports enthusiasts the opportunity strap on those new ski boots and to try out those new skis and they got for Christmas. With a little luck and a few snowflakes, kids can head for the nearest park or hillside and jump on their sleds and flyers.

For the hardcore sports fans, January offers a smorgasbord of must-see games. Professional football begins its playoff season and annual march towards the Super Bowl, our newest American holiday. More than 350 Division I College basketball teams start their conferences schedules in a quest to reach round ball Nirvana-March Madness (otherwise known as staying up until the wee hours of the morning to see how your tournament brackets are shaping up).

If you really think about it, January can be as productive, active, and as much fun as any other month that hosts any of the "big" holidays. It's what you make of January that counts. Then again, that's the case for most things in life. Happy January!

HOW DOES MY GARDEN GROW?

Published June 2018, in *PrimeTime magazine*.

The soil has been turned and fertilized. Seedlings have been planted. And with a plea to famously fickle New England weather gods, I'm hoping for a good harvest for Annual Garden 47. I can almost a taste a plateful of just-picked garden tomatoes perched on chunks of mozzarella, dressed with olive oil, balsamic vinegar, garlic and basil, complimented by slices fresh hard crusted Italian bread. Why Annual Garden 47? I guess a historic summary is in order.

I grew up in the in South Providence tenement houses. Our first floor Crary Street tenement had a cement yard. Our second floor home on Hospital Street had a small back yard with considerably more hard dirt than grass. A few odd fruit trees dotted the neighborhood and the assorted grapevines wound around backyard arbors, built by first generation Italian immigrants. Once a year, we enjoyed the sights, smells, and sounds of grapes being pressed from those arbors for potent homemade wine.

Fresh fruits and vegetables were purchased in stores, or from vendors ambling into our neighborhoods on their well-established routes. In my late Aunt Tillie's case, buying produce was a test of her bargaining skills. Many a vendor on the streets of DePasquale Avenue in Federal Hill was a victim of her superior negotiating prowess. Farms were something you saw driving by the Adult Correctional Institute (where Mulligan's Island amusement area stands today), or along Route 2 on the way to South County.

On the other hand, my wife Kathy grew up as the oldest of seven children in Woodsville, New Hampshire, a small town in the White Mountain region. Half of their back yard was dominated by a huge garden of corn, beans, tomatoes, peas, beets, potatoes, raspberries, strawberries, and assorted other vegetables and fruits. The garden provided fresh produce for her large family and considerable surplus for canning and preserving.

In 1971, we planted Annual Garden One at our first home in North Providence. The 90 year old Centredale house was one of the first built Hobson Avenue. The house sat atop a section of huge ledge that extended under most of the neighborhood. In fact, a section of our front foundation was built AROUND this ledge. The rest of the slab sloped upward to a hill outside the house that was camouflaged by grass. In later years, that hill was the venue for neighborhood daredevils (including my two sons) to pedal down at maximum speed in an attempt to become airborne, an early version of the BMX bike circuit events.

The house was bracketed by empty lots on each side. Before moving in, we had all the brush, bushes, and overgrown trees cleared and grass planted. Over the years, those plots became baseball, whiffle ball, soccer, and football fields. One of those lots was destined to become the site of Annual Garden One and the beginning of our agricultural history.

During our first spring on Hobson Avenue, Kathy decided to return to her rural roots and plant a garden. There was only one small, but significantly arduous issue with the plan. The grass had ALREADY GROWN over the potential site! Using a pick axe, shovel, and a hoe (all foreign tools to a city boy such as myself), I hacked out a space about eight feet wide and 10 feet long, bordered by all the rocks I had unearthed during the "excavation." Annual Garden One included radishes, carrots, corn, tomatoes, string beans, and sunflowers. During the ensuing weeks, after my aching muscles had healed, I warmed to the idea of becoming an urban farmer. The prospect of actually growing fresh vegetables made the tasks of weeding and daily watering less burdensome.

One evening, I spied a cluster of green sprouts in the corner of the garden. Curiosity demanded that I pull up one of the sprouts to see what it was hiding. To my amazement, there was a perfectly formed red radish dangling right there in front of me! I celebrated my agricultural triumph by brushing off the dirt and immediately devouring my discovery! Over the years, Hobson Annual Gardens Two through 17 became a little larger and yielded crops of tomatoes, eggplant, beans, zucchini, summer squash and other produce.

When we moved to our new North Providence home in 1988, we cultivated a 12 by three foot patch of ground on the side of the garage into Annual Garden 18. That section has been the site of Annual Gardens 18 through 47. Recently, Kathy added an Annex to our Annual Garden on another small piece of ground in the corner of the yard. She also cultivates a beautiful flower garden running more than 35 feet along the backyard fence.

Last year, Annual Garden 46 yielded hundreds of small grape tomatoes (Kathy likes them, but they I think it's like eating a sliver of a Snickers bar), meaty beefsteak and other varieties of larger tomatoes, bell peppers, zucchini, broccoli, Brussels sprouts (not my choice), and a few pumpkins. We gave away countless tomatoes and zucchini from the plentiful harvest. We also cooked up and froze a marinara sauce from vine-ripened tomatoes. Annual Garden 47 has much of the same lineup.

I enjoy tending the garden and watching the plants grow, flower, mature, and yield the produce. I have come to appreciate my agrarian transformation from an inner city kid to gentleman farmer. Now if you will excuse me, it's time to weed and water Annual Garden 47 and commune with my cultivating spirit.

BEACH DAYS FROM LONG AGO

Published August 2019, in *PrimeTime* magazine.

The damp, cold, windy months that pass for a New England spring are just an inconvenient stop for me on the way to summer. Summer is filled with my favorite outdoor pursuits such as golf, family get-togethers, tending to the vegetable garden, sitting in my backyard bent listening to Yankee games, or digging for quahogs in the flats at Point Judith. Summer also brings back memories of days spent at Scarborough Beach with my two closest high school friends, Gene Ripa and Joe Cambio.

On a sunny summer Saturday or Sunday one of us would commandeer the family car and set out for Scarborough, simply because that's where the high school girls hung out. The drive down to South County gave us a chance to escape from our inner city neighborhoods for a few hours. Joe lived in the heart of Federal Hill. Gene lived the middle of Silver Lake and I lived in South Providence, just a stone's throw from Rhode Island Hospital.

The conversations that took place as we rolled down Reservoir Avenue have long since faded into the past, but music by the Beatles, Rolling Stones, Herman's Hermits, the Four Seasons, the Supremes, the Mammas and the Pappas, the Beach Boys or other pop artists played on the radio. We drove by Sockanosset and the vegetable gardens tended by the inmates at the Adult Correctional Institution (where Mulligan's Island golf and amusement center now stands) on our way down Route 2 South.

Hard as it is to imagine today, barely a mile after passing the ACI, buildings and businesses became more scattered. The Warwick Mall would not open until 1970 and the next landmark you would reach was the Warwick Musical Theatre (The Tent). The theatre (on the site of a Lowe's superstore today) fell silent in 1999; but for more than 40 years the Bonoff family owned the theater and booked road companies staging Broadway musicals and brought headliners such as Buddy Hackett,

Sammy Davis, Jr., Connie Francis, Don Rickles, Joan Rivers, Wayne Newton, and Liberace to the Rhode Island entertainment scene.

After passing The Tent, the landscape became even more rural until you reached the vast rolling hills, in front of the Bostitch Staple Company. A car dealership sits next to that factory now; but for a trio of beach bound teenagers, that immense lawn marked a significant point in our trip. We were getting closer to the beach. We had left much of civilization behind.

When you passed a Native American Museum, you knew that the Route 4 Rotary was just ahead. Turning onto Route 1 from Route 4, our destination seemed tantalizingly close. The only thing standing in our way now was the weekend beach traffic crawl. When we drove on to the access road to Scarborough, the smell of the ocean foretold a day at the shore.

After we found a parking space (free in those days), it was time to stake out a spot for our beach blankets. The base of operations satisfied two objectives. It had to be close enough to the water to swim or body surf and also serve as a central location for walks in any direction along the shore to look for friends or watch the girls stroll by. Occasionally, we would cross the invisible barrier that separated Scarborough from the private Olivo's Beach, where the older crowd hung out drinking beer and playing their music at a decibel level that got your attention. That would be us some day, we speculated.

About 5:00 p.m. we would shake out the blankets, stash them in the trunk, and begin the ride home. It wasn't long before we were swallowed up by the line of traffic snaking along the beach route leading back to the city. The trip home always seemed to be longer and more tedious. The anticipation that had built up on our way the beach had dissipated. The only thing that alleviated our negative vibes was knowing that sunny weather next weekend would bring us back to the beach to resume our summer rituals.

When I sit in summer traffic on my way to the South County shore today, I recall those beach days of the past. The landscape along Route 2 has changed dramatically. The ACI vegetable gardens are gone. Malls, fast food restaurants and all sorts of commercial and retail outlets are jammed together like Fig Newtons packed in a row and sealed in package of never ending traffic signals. The Warwick Musical Theater, Bostitch, Native American Museum and the Route 4 Rotary are just images stored in the recesses of my memory bank now. But if I feel the need, I can revive these landmarks at any time, particularly during those damp, cool, windy days that pass for a New England spring.

A CHRISTMAS GIFT EVERY DAY

Published December 2008, in *PrimeTime magazine*.

We've all heard the adage, "Man plans and God laughs." As in life, it's the truth when it comes to freelance writing. Like many writers, I keep a notebook to jot down idea, phrases, or inspirations for future columns, lest they be lost in the noise of everyday comings and goings. Occasionally, life events supplant those inspirations and what's on the docket for that month's *PRIME-TIME* column. This is one of those months. So you'll have to wait a little bit longer for "You Can't Make it Up, Chapter II."

This summer, doctors discovered a small mass on my left kidney. Initially, there was some question as to whether the mass was malignant or not. However, CAT scans and other tests revealed that the mass was cancerous. This was not the first time I had heard the diagnosis of cancer. In 2008, my bladder and prostate had been removed in a six-hour operation at Massachusetts General Hospital in Boston.

Thanks to the skills of that talented surgical team in Boston, I have lived normally for the last 11 years, with very few lifestyle changes. I have watched my twin 16-year old granddaughters Kailyn and Sophia, and their 10-year brother Nicholas, grow and prosper. Last year, my son and daughter-in-law welcomed a new baby boy, Benjamin Dale, Jr. into our family. Kathy and I (we celebrated 49 years of marriage in November) have enjoyed many adventures including a cross-county drive in 2015, a trips France and Ireland, a family vacation in the Caribbean, and a cruise through the Panama Canal. For the last four years, we escaped the New England winter spending a few months in Florida. We have written two books together.

Looking back, I realized that have received many gifts in the last 11 years. You could say that I've been favored with Christmas gifts every month of each year since my first cancer operation in November 2008. Those gifts of family, friends, love, support, and a strong spiritual foundation are truly priceless.

That being said, a diagnosis of cancer always carries with it an implied aura of human mortality. The stark reality of one of the world's most dreaded and powerful diseases is a cloud that instantly alters your perspective and places the rest of your life in physical and psychological limbo.

While initial analysis of tests indicated that only part of my kidney might need to be removed, surgeon Dr. Dragan Golijanin prepared us for the possibility of there being "more than meets the eye" when surgery was performed. Perhaps the entire kidney would have to be removed. The silver lining was that surgery would preclude the need for any additional treatment such as chemotherapy or radiation. I felt very fortunate that my first cancer surgery did not require any aftercare either.

At 6:00 a.m. on October 7, Kathy and I showed up at the Miriam Hospital surgical registration desk. I remember hoping that the surgical team had at least one cup of coffee in them by then. At 7:00 a.m., I was wheeled into the pre-op wing for final surgery preparations. At that point, I began the constant repetition of reciting my name and birthday to a squadron of nurses, interns, physician assistants, and doctors in Golijanin's team, the anesthesiologist and anyone else who asked. I was convinced that I would surrender my name and birthday to the sanitary engineer if he asked.

Finally, they marked my abdomen and I was transported into the theatre of operation. I glanced over to the console where Dr. Golijanin would take the controls of a robot that would assist him in the surgery. I remember hoping that he had been extremely good at X-Box when he was a kid. After one last round of identifications, the final dose of anesthesia was administered and I entered the Twilight Zone.

During the five-hour procedure, Dr. Goljanin discovered that the mass on my kidney was deeper and more extensive than originally thought. My entire kidney was removed. When the extent of the surgery was revealed to us, my wry sense of humor clicked in to note that I didn't have too many spare parts left.

My recovery has been a bit slower than I would have liked; but patience was never one of my more developed character traits. The long recovery has given me a chance to remember two necessary elements of a contented and mindful life… appreciation and gratitude. I have vowed to appreciate and be grateful for the gifts of family, friends, health, and solid spiritual beliefs. I realize that I receive precious and invaluable Christmas gifts every day… the gift of life and another chance to live it one day at a time.

I wish you a very joyous and peaceful Holiday Season and best wishes for a happy, healthy, and productive New Year.

SPORTING LIFE

TAKE ME OUT TO THE BALLGAME

Published March 2016, in PrimeTime magazine.

I 've always viewed March 1 as a psychological turning point in the battle against winter. Baseball's spring training season is in full swing. And when my thoughts turn to hits, runs, stolen bases, and no-hitters, anticipation runs high at the prospect of yet another road trip.

The annual Nancy LaVoice Baseball and Cultural Tour (I'll explain later) was born on a cold late September afternoon game at Wrigley Field in 1999 with the St. Louis Cardinals playing the Chicago Cubs. My brother-in-law Tommy and his wife Nancy, Kathy and I had decided to make the pilgrimage to the Mecca of major league ball yards earlier that spring. As any true baseball fan knows, Wrigley is a required visit for any diamond aficionado. Other stops would include the legendary Fenway Park, Yankee Stadium, and the model for all "retro" stadiums, Oriole Park at Camden Yards.

The plan was to take in a game at all major league stadiums. The rules were simple. We set up a four-person "starting rotation" and would visit the ballpark of that person's choice. A couple of years later, my brother-in-law Peter and my son Benjamin were added to the bullpen as relievers with full selection rights.

Everyone was assigned a role in planning the trips. Kathy and Nancy were in charge of hotels, tours, and cultural activities in each city. Originally, Tommy was in charge of ticket purchases. Tommy is legendary for his thriftiness, so I fired him a few years into the tour because we were tired of sitting in stadium third decks!

Unfortunately, Nancy passed away in 2010. In tribute to her decade long contributions, we decided to name the tour in honor of her memory. When Tommy re-married two years ago, Darlene joined the team.

Baseball is a complicated, random yet precise, rhythmic, pastoral game played in parks tucked into the hearts of urban hubs. Each sequence of play begins with a silent, secretive, elaborate selection process involving the pitcher and the catcher trying to create the perfect pitch to fool the batter. This decision is affected by factors such as perceived weaknesses in the batter's swing, the number of outs, who is on base, the inning, and the score. Simultaneously, the batter is trying to calculate the type and speed of the pitch and where he wants to hit the ball.

Fielders move according to the type of pitch to be thrown, where the hitter tends to drive the ball, and where they have the best option of throwing him, or a runner, out at what base. Defensive and offensive strategies are orchestrated by a manager sitting on a bench. The plan of attack is relayed to a coach on the field who signals the manager's strategies to the players in a messaging ritual that resembles the mating dance of a praying mantis. This sequence is repeated approximately 300 times a game in about 15 seconds!

To date, the Nancy LaVoice Baseball and Cultural Tour has stopped in Arlington, Baltimore, Chicago (White Sox and Cubs), Cincinnati, Cleveland, Denver, Detroit, Houston, Kansas City, Los Angeles (Angels and Dodgers), Milwaukee, Phoenix, Pittsburgh, St. Louis, San Diego, San Francisco, Seattle, Toronto, and Washington, D.C.

We make it a point to tour each of the cities we visit. My favorite stops are Fisherman's Wharf in San Francisco, Pike's Peak in Colorado, the Public Market in Seattle, Motown Museum in Detroit, the Truman Museum and the Negro Baseball Hall of Fame in Kansas City, the Underground Railroad Museum in Cincinnati, the Untouchables Mob Tour and Navy Pier in Chicago, the Rock and Roll Hall of Fame in Cleveland, and witnessing a cattle drive through the streets of Fort Worth.

We have sampled Highline chili in Cincinnati, ribs in Kansas City, crabs in Baltimore and San Francisco, salmon in Seattle, Italian beef sandwiches in Chicago, Primanti sandwiches in Pittsburgh, beer and bratwurst in Milwaukee, ribs and beer in St. Louis, steaks in Texas, and chops in Denver. My mouth still can taste the Ghirardelli chocolates in San Francisco. There are clam rolls in Boston, cheese steaks in

Philadelphia, cheese cakes in New York, and pecan pies in Atlanta to be devoured.

I don't know what new itinerary we will develop we when we compete the Nancy LaVoice Baseball and Cultural Tour. Whatever adventure we embark on, it will be a celebration of history, culture, sights, sounds, smells, and tastes. Thanks, Nancy.

FORE... FIVE... SIX... OR MORE!

Published August 2016, in PrimeTime magazine.

DISCLAIMER: *Any similarities between my golf game and the game as played by pros on the PGA Tour is purely coincidental.*

According to Mark Twain, "Golf is a good walk spoiled." Some days, I think he's right. Other days, I remember former President Gerald Ford saying, "I know I'm getting better at golf because I'm hitting fewer spectators." In my case, I'm hitting fewer golfers playing in the opposite fairway.

My golfing "career," began at about age 12, when a family friend we called Uncle Eddie, gave me wooden shaft golf clubs with rusted heads. I scrapped the rust off with scouring pads and polished the shafts. In retrospect, it would have been wiser to recondition the clubs, stash them away for a few years, and sell them later as antiques. But I'm getting ahead of myself.

Uncle Eddie owned a home in Swansea, Massachusetts surrounded by vast acres of open land; a pond fully equipped with a dock and stocked with fish, and inhabited by a large colony of frogs; all bordered by a small forest of pine trees. During one of our many visits, I was practicing my golf swing in the back yard and sent a ball smashing through a huge plate glass window in their family room. Fortunately, Uncle Eddie owned glass shop, so my parents only had to pay for replacement materials. At the moment of shattering impact, I should have understood the message that the golf gods were sending. But I'm still getting ahead of myself.

I played my first rounds at Silver Spring in East Providence, a six-hole course wedged between the Providence River tank farms and Pawtucket Avenue. During one of these early rounds, I somehow executed a flawless swing and plopped a ball about two inches from the hole. More than 50 years have passed. I've played hundreds of times. And that's still the closest I've ever come to golfing perfection-a hole-in-one! While we're talking about the hole-in-one, could somebody explain the strangely backward tradition where the golfer who shoots a hole-in-one has to buy everyone in the clubhouse a drink? Shouldn't it be the other way around?

I did not have the chance, nor the inclination to play in my teenage years. When I went to work in 1970 at the old Davol Rubber plant in Providence, I bought a set of used clubs and joined the company golf league. Once again, I tried to master this incredibly frustrating and exasperating sport. As a fellow hacker once declared after a particularly disastrous hole, "If you want to learn humility, play golf.

After a few years of hacking at golf courses across the state, countless tossed clubs, questionable language, and mounting aggravation, I sold the clubs and quit the game. I'd had enough. Consistency was an elusive goal. On one occasion, my scorecard showed a three-hole sequence of 10, two, and 10 strokes. I also realized that raising three children could be aggravating enough, and it was free! Hence, I would be saving money and simultaneously lowering my blood pressure.

After a hiatus of more than 20 years I decided to take up the game again. I bought another set of used clubs and was determined not to repeat the mistakes of the past. So I took lessons. Once again, I ignored a loud and clear message from the golf gods. During my first lesson, the instructor told me to take a practice swing so he could judge my level of incompetency. After witnessing my swing, he took a step back from the practice tee and announced that I had very little chance of succeeding! Despite the instructor's dire predictions, I've spent the last 15 years playing regularly with a group of friends that are willing to ignore my golfing goofs.

About 10 years ago, my wife Kathy decided to take up the game. She asked me to teach her and I suggested that she take lessons. I knew that all I would be illustrating would be my bad habits. She heeded my advice and took lessons from a local golf pro. As a result, she hits the ball much straighter than I do. While I may achieve greater distance with my imperfect swing, I go searching through the woods for my misguided missile many more times than she does.

Today, I play with a TaylorMade graphite shaft oversized driver and Callaway irons safely secured in a Nike deluxe golf bag. My scores have not improved significantly, but I look better on the first tee.

Over the years, my attitude concerning golf has changed significantly. We play for the entertainment and exercise. We play for the adventure; we never know what is going to happen. We play for the camaraderie, the inevitable kibitzing, and the frequent bursts of laughter. We play for that one hole where a combination of luck and a few good shots give the illusion that we know what we are doing. Bob Hope's once declared, "I'll shoot my age if I live to be 105." My links philosophy can be summed up by paraphrasing a bit of popular advice, "Keep Calm and Tee It Up."

NOTE: *I am STILL, to paraphrase Mark Twain, "ruining a good walk."*

SANDWICHED IN
A FOOTBALL RIVALRY

Published February 2017, in PrimeTime magazine.

On Sunday, February 5, tens of millions of people will turn on their big screen televisions, many that may have been purchased just for this event, to join in an unofficial national holiday, Super Bowl Sunday. This year, the 51st Super Bowl to determine the National Football League champions will be held in Houston, Texas. No doubt, many fans of the winning team may miss work on Monday after celebrating victory and many fans of the losing team will proclaim "Wait until next year."

For more years than I can remember, I have been sandwiched in the middle of a rivalry between my two sons. Matt is a New York Giants fan and Ben is a Dallas Cowboy rooter. I am a Giants fan. Since the teams are in the same division, they play each other twice every year. If they may meet in a playoff game, to determine which team goes to the Super Bowl, I will be faced with a dilemma. I face the same situation when my alma mater, URI plays PC, a team I have rooted for since the 1970s. Trying to stay almost neutral in either situation is difficult.

As of this year, Ben holds a slight edge in Super Bowl bragging rights. The Cowboys have won five championships and the Giants have won four. In my case, I quietly revel in the two Giants two Super Bowl victories over the Patriots because I live in North Providence, the heart of Patriot and Tom Brady nation.

I became a fan of the Giants in 1958 while watching the NFL championship game between the Baltimore (at the time) Colts and the Giants on my uncle's basement television. Although Alan Ameche's touchdown plunge from the one yard line in overtime gave the Colts a 23-17 victory, that game made me a Giants fan. That epic battle was tabbed as the Greatest Game Ever Played and was instrumental in stirring interest in the NFL.

After that, I watched every game that was broadcast in my area. The Giants were the closest NFL team to Providence. Most games were televised since the Giants sold out all home games in Yankee in Stadium and road games were always on television. The Patriots did not begin play until 1960 in the upstart American Football League. In 1969, the AFL merged with the NFL. By then, my loyalty was set.

During the 1960s, Shell gas stations would hand out free black and white reproduction drawings of a different Giants player each week if you bought eight gallons of gas. I remember collecting sketches of team stars Frank Gifford, Pat Summerall, Y.A. Tittle, Del Shofner, Bob Schnelker, and Sam Huff.

Matt began rooting for the Giants as soon as he became a football fan. We celebrated their first Super Bowl win over the Denver Broncos in 1986 and held our breath in 1991 as Scott Norwood missed a 48-yard field goal to seal a Giants victory. We also remember the infamous helmet catch by David Tryee to help the Giants win in 2008 and the pinpoint pass to Mario Manningham to set up the 2012 championship.

Ben's history is a little more circumspect. He started out as a Tony Dorsett and Dallas Cowboy fan. When Dorsett went from the Cowboys to the Denver Broncos, he adopted the Broncos. When Dorsett retired from football, Ben returned to rooting for the Cowboys. Christmas photos of years gone by show them wearing the new jerseys of each of the three teams at one point or another.

When Ben resumed his allegiance to the Dallas Cowboys, a friendly sibling rivalry with his brother Matt, complete with the customary verbal jousting, was under way. In fact, when the Cowboys and Giants meet twice a year, they usually observe what amounts to "radio silence" for a week until the details of the game are digested. This season, the Giants beat the Cowboys twice, but they were just a prelude to the playoffs.

For the first time in a few years, both teams are in the playoffs. Since they are in the same conference, they cannot both play in the Super Bowl, but they might meet in Dallas to determine which team gets to play in that pigskin extravaganza. If that happens, I will be sandwiched between their two rooting interests once again.

MORE THAN 50 YEARS OF YANKEE MEMORIES

Published July 2017, in PrimeTime magazine.

The New York Yankees hosted their 71st annual Old Timers Day on June 25. This tradition, first held in 1947, brings out retired Yankee players, coaches, and managers to the Yankee Stadium. Old Timers Day gives these former Yankees a chance to share stories about their careers and the team's rich history. While my memories of Old Timers Day are tucked in my baseball mind, you should know the origins of my rooting interests.

Following the leanings of my father and uncles, I was a Red Sox fan. In 1960, I was 11 and had become increasingly disheartened by the bumbling Red Sox, so I committed the ultimate act of treason-I became a Yankee fan.

All that summer, I strained to listen to the scratchy signals of Yankee broadcasts to follow my newly adopted team. It was particularly funny to listen to former Yankee shortstop "The Scooter" Phil Rizzuto describe the game. Since Phil's mind frequently wandered and began to talk his playing days, his wife's cooking, or the traffic on the George Washington Bridge, he would forget the score, the count on the batter, who was on base, and how many outs there were. Bill White, his broadcasting sidekick, had the job of keeping The Scooter on task. Phil was very content with his play-by-play style and White achieved only minimal success.

When the Yankees lost the Game Seven of the 1960 World Series on Bill Mazerowski's winning home run to crown the Pittsburgh Pirates as baseball's champions, I was crushed. I wondered if I was a baseball jinx. At age 11, sports wounds heal quickly and the 1961 season was legendary for a team that already possessed a remarkable sports history. The resurgent Bronx Bombers belted 240 homers , lead by Roger Maris with 61 and Mickey Mantle with 54, and ripped though the schedule hammering opponents to win the American League pennant and one of their 27 World Series titles. I was a Yankee fan forever.

My first trip to the Big Ballpark in the Bronx was Old Timers Day on July 29, 1978. The Yanks were in the midst of a raucous season marked by personality conflicts and fueled by the combative personality of their manager Billy Martin. Martin has been fired earlier by the equally combative owner George Steinbrenner (one of five hirings and firings in the Martin-Steinbrenner Continuing Soap Opera).

For the rest of the 1978 season, Bob Lemon managed the team in the team and guided them to a first place, erasing a deficit of more than 14 games. On October 8, the Yanks met you-know-who at you-know what Park in a one game playoff. The Yankee victory was highlighted (unless you a Red Sox fan) by a three-run homer by you-know-who (Bucky Dent).

In 1978, Old Timers Day included Mickey Mantle and Whitey Ford among many others. At the 1973 Old Timers Game, Mickey Mantle hit home run off his old teammate Whitey Ford. It was his last home run.

The 1978 ceremonies featured a surprise guest. It was announced that Billy Martin would return as Yankee manager in 1980. The Stadium shook with applause.

The only former player who was upset was Yankee legend Joe Di-Maggio. He always demanded to be introduced last. The miffed Di-Maggio made it pompously clear that, in the future, he would have to give advance approval of any player introduced after him, or he would not attend. Other Yankee stars at Old Timers Days over the years included Yogi Berra, Rizzuto, Don Larsen Reggie Jackson, Paul O'Neil, Joe Torre, David Wells, Ron Guidry, and Tino Martinez, to name a few.

Yankee Stadium was a fascinating park where it seemed that baseball lore was created every year. The atmosphere whispers the timeless achievements of the great New York players and teams of the past.

I have seen games at Fenway Park and Wrigley Field in Chicago and the both have undeniable baseball charm. Fenway has the Green Monster left field wall just an inviting 315 feet from home plate, its deep cavern in center field, and the famous Pesky Pole a mere 302 feet from home plate. Over the years, The Wall has probably taken away as many home runs as it has given up, but the smartest BoSox hitters have learned to use the Green Monster to their advantage.

Wrigley Field sits in the middle of a lively neighborhood, and can boast of ivy covered walls jutting out to an oddly shaped right field corner, a hand-operated score board, and rabid bleacher fans. A baseball game at Wrigley Field is not just game, it is a social experience!

Today, Fenway fans sing Sweet Caroline in the 8th inning. Wrigley fans wait patiently for the traditional guest soloist to sing Take Me Out to the Ballgame. But Yankee right field bleacher creatures have their own tradition known as the Roll Call. As each Yankee player takes his position at the start of the game, the fans chant their names until the player acknowledges the cheers with a wave or tip of the cap. Former right fielder Nick Swisher was more dramatic as he turned to them and snapped off a salute.

I have seen three notable games at Yankee Stadium. I sat in a right field seat on October 26, 1996 when the Yankees beat the Atlanta Braves in Game 6 to capture their first World Series title in 18 years. Wade Boggs, a Red Sox refugee, celebrated the title by riding around the field on horseback with a New York City policeman as his pilot.

I was in the left field stands on October 16, 2003 when you-know-who (Aaron Boone) hit an extra inning home run in the epic Game 7 of the 2003 League Championship Series. I had the good fortune to be in a luxury box on September 26, 2013 when Mariano Rivera, the greatest relief pitcher of all time with 652 saves, came in to pitch for the last time in his career to the strains of Enter Sandman by Metallica.

I have great Yankee Stadium memories. I just hope that my father and uncles, wherever they are, have forgiven me by now.

RHODE ISLAND'S SILVER SLUGGERS KEEP SWINGING

Published August 2018, in PrimeTime magazine.

E very Wednesday morning from late April through late August, six tribes gather at neatly groomed and lined diamonds at Warwick's City Park to repeat a ritual most of them have honored over the span of many decades. At 9:15 a.m., battle tested warriors in their 60s, 70s, 80s, and one intrepid 90-year old take positions on the diamonds waiting for the first pitch to be arced towards the batter. Warwick Senior Slow Pitch Softball double-headers are underway.

This is my third season in the league. I began playing softball in 1972 with the Davol Rubber team in the old Industrial League. With the exception of seven or eight seasons, I've been a pitcher, catcher, first baseman, middle man (over second base), and occasional outfielder for teams in twilight, night, and Sunday morning leagues. I even made a guest appearance on a New Hampshire team in a Vermont Labor Day tournament several years ago. I have played in hundreds of games on dozens of fields and Warwick Senior Softball is the most fun I've had playing ball in many years.

The league has given me a chance to rejoin former teammates and compete once again with old rivals. While a few players are still active in more competitive settings, the perspectives we bring to the game today are distinctly different from past contests tucked into our softball memory banks. The emphasis today focuses on enjoying the sunshine, getting some exercise, and engaging in the time-honored tradition of kibitzing.

The Wednesday slow-pitch softball rules are different from those of more traditional leagues. We use a wooden platform at home plate to determine balls and strikes. If the ball hits the platform, it's a strike. We umpire our own games; keep our scores without the aid of an electronic scoreboard, and are very liberal regarding the use of courtesy runners. With some of our older players, a substitute runner leaves home plate and sprints (or what passes for sprinting at our age) towards first base on bat/ball contact. Rules prohibit throwing a runner out at first base from the outfield on a base hit and outfielders position themselves behind plastic cones placed 150 feet from home before each pitch. Every out on the base paths is a force out.

For safety, runners must touch a first base bag placed on the side of the official base. Runners score by touching a home plate stationed a few feet outside and parallel to the official home plate. You are allowed to score only five runs an inning until the 7th "open" inning. In an open inning, the trailing team can score as many runs as it can to win or tie the game. Sometimes we create our own rules. On one particularly hot summer morning with the score tied after seven innings, we agreed to start the next game rather than break the tie.

All players are listed in a continuous batting lineup and are free to go in and out of any defensive position at any time. Players frequently share defensive spots during a game. To assure that all players get an equal opportunity to hit, the batting rotation picks up in the second game of the doubleheader where the lineup ended in the previous game. On occasion, this ironic diamond twist allows players like me, who are often accused of running with a pianos strapped to our backs, to become lead-off hitters!

Many of the traits and abilities displayed by players in their younger years are still evident today. The power hitters of yesteryear are today's silver sluggers. The jackrabbits of earlier days are still speedsters. Well known kibitzers have polished their repertoire of baseball jabs and retained their ability to turn out snappy phrases seasoned with humor.

No standings are kept; there's no year-end tournament to crown a league champion; and we don't name a league's Most Valuable Player. At the season ending pizza party, the year's highlights are embellished and bloopers are exaggerated.

After all the innings are played, there is a unanimous consensus about the season. Warwick Senior Softballers are happy to be healthy enough to play and enjoy a game we love. We revel in the camaraderie. We are staying active and celebrating the American baseball tradition.

If the ritual repeats itself, we'll begin our "spring training" sometime in March...or maybe not. It's much more likely that a few days before the season starts we'll rummage through the closet or go into the garage, find our bats, balls, and gloves, (AND the compression pants and assorted braces), and show up for opening day. We'll jog at bit; stretch a bit; take a few silver slugger practice swings and announce that we are ready for the season. Play ball!

WOONSOCKET'S CLEM LABINE WAS A DIAMOND GEM AMONG THE LEGENDARY BOYS OF SUMMER

Published September 2018, in PrimeTime magazine.

I n the 1972 book "The Boys of Summer," Roger Kahn revived the memories of older baseball fans and introduced a new generation of fans to Ebbets Field and legendary Brooklyn Dodgers of the 1950s. "Dem Bums," as the team was named by local sports reporters, captured the World Series championship in 1955 and sewed the names of icons such as Pee Wee Reese, Jackie Robinson, Don Newcomb, Duke Snider, Roy Campanella, Gil Hodges, Preacher Roe, Carl Erskine, among others into the fabric of baseball history. Dodger hurler and Rhode Islander Clement Walter (Clem) Labine holds a prominent place in that championship season.

Labine was born in Lincoln on August 6, 1926. He was the son of a weaver, a common occupation for French Canadian immigrants of the era, but lived in Woonsocket. Labine returned to Woonsocket at the end of each baseball season to work as a sports clothing designer and later as general manager of the of the Jacob Finklestein and Sons Manufacturing Company sports apparel division. Labine died at age 80 on March 2, 2007 in Vero Beach, Florida after suffering two strokes during hospitalization for pneumonia. At the time of his passing, he was a celebrity coach at the Dodger Fantasy Camp.

Clem Labine pitched in the major leagues from 1951 through 1962. Most of his major league career was spent with the Brooklyn, then Los Angeles Dodgers. He also pitched for the Detroit Tigers, Pittsburgh Pirates and the expansion New York Mets in 1962. Labine was a two-time All Star and three-time World Champion, having won in 1955 with Brooklyn, 1959 with the Los Angeles Dodgers, and 1960 with the Pittsburgh Pirates. (The 1960 championship was a year of extreme personal distress. Pittsburgh's Bill Mazerowski homered the 9th inning of the Series' seventh game to send my newly-adopted favorite team, the

New York Yankees to defeat). It wasn't the first time Labine's career would intersect with baseball history

Clem's widow, Barbara (Todisco-Gershkoff) Labine was born in Providence and now lives in Lincoln. One room in Barbara's home is devoted to mementos of her husband's distinguished career. Walking into that room magically transports you into Brooklyn Dodger and Clem Labine's legacies. A glass tabletop supported by three legs made of Clem's bats sits in the middle of the room. Perched on the tabletop are Clem's baseball glove, a replica of Ebbets Field, and a 1957 World Series pay stub encased in Lucite. Sketches drawn by the late Providence Journal illustrator, Frank Lanning, a framed collection of photographs celebrating moments of Dodger history featuring Labine with luminaries such as Robinson, Snider, Reese, and others, and several newspaper clippings chronicling Labine's achievements adorn the walls. One wall displays a cover of the June 3, 1957 Sports Illustrated cover proclaiming him as King of the Bullpen.

Barbara met Clem at while golfing at the Kirkbrae Country club in Lincoln in 1980. They married in 1982. Clem had lost his first wife, also named Barbara, a few years earlier. When Barbara was introduced to Labine, she had no idea that he was a former Major Leaguer. "As a kid, I would spend Saturdays at my grandmother's house listening to the New York Metropolitan Opera, so I didn't know much about baseball," she laughs.

Labine had four children with his first wife. Clem Labine Junior, died in 2012. A United States Marine Corp veteran, he had lost his leg in a landmine explosion while on duty in Vietnam. They also had a daughter, Barbara Grubbs of Reno, and twins Gail Polanski and Kim Archambault of Smithfield. The Labine clan also included Barbara's daughter, Susan Gershkoff of Lincoln.

While Barbara wasn't initially aware of her husband's storied diamond career, the baseball world certainly knew. Labine pitched in 538 major league games, the majority as a reliever. His competitive nature drove him to relish bullpen work. He told Dodger pitcher and teammate Carl Erskine, "I don't want to start. I liked the pressure of coming into the game with everything on the line." There was no save statistic during his career; but he was awarded 96 career saves retroactively when the "save" category became an official baseball statistic. In his major league career, Labine won 77 games and lost 56, with a 3.63 earned run average. Ironically, two of Labine's best performances came as a starter. The significance of these two starts is partially obscured by the shadows of two of baseball's most iconic moments.

In 1951, the Brooklyn Dodgers and New York Giants (later of San Francisco) ended the season tied for first place in the National League. The winner of a three-game playoff would win the pennant and go on to the World Series. The Giants had won the first game. Dodger Rookie Labine, whose 13 wins included 10 out of the bullpen, was tabbed to pitch the second game to keep Brooklyn's title hopes alive. Labine threw a brilliant six-hit shutout in the Dodger 10 to nothing win, baffling the Giants with his trademark curve balls and sinkers. That game, however, was destined to be a prelude to the dramatic third game. The Giants five to four victory was highlighted by Bobby Thompson's legendary "shot heard around the world" homer that broke the four to four deadlock.

On October 9, 1956, Labine was named the Dodger starter in Game Six of the World Series against the New York Yankees. If the Dodgers lost, the World Series championship would be claimed by their crosstown imperial and hated rivals. Labine seven-hit the Yankees in a 10-inning, one to nothing win. The Yankees won the seventh game and the Series crown the next day in a 10 to nothing shutout. Labine's masterpiece was overshadowed by Yankee Don's Larsen's perfect game two to nothing win hurled the previous day.

While Labine was a confident, some say cocky, pitcher who achieved significant diamond success, he is remembered as kind, considerate, and generous by those who knew him. In 1955, Labine spearheaded fundraising relief efforts for hometown Woonsocket after two major hurricanes had pushed the Blackstone River over its banks to flood he city. Barbara noted that he always took time to talk with fans and sign autographs, even if he was in the middle of meal. "He was a real gentleman," Barbara mused. "He always stood up when a lady entered the room." When Labine died, Hall of Fame Dodger broadcaster

Vin Scully remarked, "He had the heart of a lion and the intelligence of a wily fox. And he was a nice guy too."

Dodger Blue still runs deep for Barbara and she talks with former Dodger wives occasionally. Relaxing in her recliner for our interview, Barbara sported a t-shirt declaring, "If you lead a good life, say your prayers, and go to church, when you die you will go to Dodgertown." No doubt, Clement Walter Labine resides in Dodgertown.

A FORTY-FIVE FOOT HEAVE INTO RHODE ISLAND BASKETBALL HISTORY

Published February 2019, in PrimeTime magazine.

I t wasn't quite David and Goliath, or the Rhode Island version of the Hickory Huskers in the film "Hoosiers," but it was a historic heave into the annals of Providence College basketball. The inspiration for this column flashed across my mind as I watched the Providence College Friars battle the Texas Longhorns in Austin. Did the Ocean State's fanatic fascination with the Friars really begin more than 60 years ago? How did a school with an undergraduate enrollment of approximately 4,000 arrive at this moment, taking the court against the University of Texas, with undergraduate population of more than 40,000?

Many Friar loyal rooters are unaware how the PC basketball mania began. The phenomenon traces its roots to a sudden jolt of good fortune on a winter night long ago. Construction of Alumni Hall, the 3,000 seat on-campus home of PC from 1956 to 1972, was completed in 1955. Providence College invited the mighty University of Notre Dame to help christen its new home on February 14, 1956. The game ended in an improbable 85 to 83 overtime Friar victory that evening. But the real story was the Herculean 45-foot winning heave to the basket by Gordie Holmes as time expired. It's a sure bet that neither Holmes, PC coach Joe Mullaney, nor the fans in attendance that night knew they were witnessing the birth of a magical six-decade run that has thrilled countless Rhode Island college basketball fans.

In 1965, I sat in the crowded, cozy confines of Alumni Hall and watched Friar basketball wizard Jimmy Walker spin, swirl, dribble, and shoot his way around, through, and over bewildered Duquesne University defenders. That was the only game I saw in the Alumni Hall setting, but I listened to many Friar basketball games on my small transistor radio. The late Chris Clark broadcast the action so vividly that you could almost see the Friars pulling out those last minute victories.

As college basketball fans in these parts know, the Friars won prestigious National Invitation Tournament titles in 1961 and 1963 (before March Madness became a media frenzy), and made Final Four appearances in 1973 and 1987. In 1961, fans lined up starting at the Connecticut border to cheer the team on its bus ride back to the PC campus. For many years, Head Coach Joe sported license plates NIT 61 and NIT 63. Mullaney's basketball journey and his innovative strategies eventually landed him a job as head coach of the Los Angeles Lakers. Mullaney ended his coaching career with a second stint as the Friar mentor.

Over the years, the Friars have rewarded their fans' loyalty with many lasting memories. My favorites are the Blizzard of 1978 triumph over North Carolina, 1979 double overtime victory against then number one Michigan and the 1997 win over Duke.

In 1979, Próvidence College became a charter member of the new Big East Conference. The conference was the brainchild of Dave Gavitt, PC basketball coach, visionary and first Big East commissioner. He predicted the rise of the power basketball conference. Original league members were PC, St. John's, Syracuse, Georgetown, Seton Hall, the University of Connecticut, and Boston College. The seven-member fledgling league also boasted college coaching legends such as John Thompson, PJ Carlissimo, Jim Boeheim, Lou Carnesecca, and Jim Calhoun. The exclusion of the University of Rhode Island has given rise to a basketball morality play re-enacted each year in the PC-URI grudge match.

Gavitt coached PC to an NCAA Final Four in 1973 and became an influential member of the USA Basketball organization. In recognition of his remarkable accomplishments, Gavitt is enshrined in the National Basketball Hall of Fame in Springfield, Massachusetts. He is joined in the Hall by PC basketball greats Lenny Wilkins and John Thompson, and Rick Pitino, who led the Friars on shocking run to an NCAA Final Four slot in 1987.

In addition to Walker, the NBA's first draft choice in 1967, the roster of former Friars who have played in the NBA (in no particular order) includes Thompson, Wilkins, Ernie Degregorio, Marvin Barnes, Mar-Shon Brooks, Otis Thorpe, Joe Hassett, Kris Dunn, Kevin Stacom, Ryan Gomes, Johnny Egan, Dickey Simpkins (owner of multiple championship rings as a player on the Michael Jordan lead Chicago Bulls), Mike Riordan, Austin Croshere, God Shammgod, and many others who enjoyed stints in the league. All of them followed that sudden trail blazed by Gordon Holmes and his 45-foot last-second launch to the basket.

FULL DISCLOSURE: *I am a graduate of the University of Rhode Island. Rhody has its own unique place in basketball history. The legendary URI coach Frank Keaney is acknowledged as the architect of modern day run and shoot, fast break basketball.*

LEGENDARY URI COACH FRANK KEANEY PUT COLLEGE BASKETBALL ON THE FAST TRACK

Published March 2019, in *PrimeTime magazine*.

The brief, unpredictable meteorological mayhem of February has passed and a wild season of sports frenzy lurks around the corner. This three-week college basketball spectacle will produce countless hours of lost worksite productivity and immeasurable hours of lost sleep as fans struggle to stay awake for those last few opening round games of the West Regional.

Some will know the agony of defeat as their tournament bracket predictions are smashed by wins of teams they barely know. Some will exalt the in the thrill of victory by picking upsets of basketball blue bloods by much smaller colleges with minimal hoops "street cred," such as last year's shocking conquest by the University of Maryland Baltimore County over top-seeded Atlantic Coast Conference giant, the University of Virginia. New media stars, such as 98-year old celestial cheerleader, Sister Jean Dolores Schmidt, patron saint of the University of Loyola Chicago Final Four squad, will streak across the tournament landscape.

Welcome to the Holy Grail of the NCAA Division I college basketball championships-the annual Roman circus of March Madness.

As you watch players streak up the court, defy gravity with rim-shattering dunks, and fire long range missiles, keep in mind that the dawn of fast-break, fast-paced college round ball began more than 70 years ago right here in Rhode Island. This round-ball revolution was the brainchild of University of Rhode Island (then Rhode Island State) coach Frank Keaney.

In the 1930s, Frank Keaney, a quirky chemistry professor who quoted Greek philosophers in team pep talks, dragged basketball out of its plodding, laborious Dark Ages into the era of point-a –minute (or more) offensive strategy. Keaney's teams would push the ball up court as fast as possible and hoist as many shots as possible. The results were both amazing and exciting. In the 1940s, URI averaged 81 points a game-30 more than any other NCAA five!

In the 1940s, the Runnin' Rams collected three invitations to the eight-team National Invitation Tournament at Madison Square Garden in New York City. The NIT was the most prestigious college basketball tournament of its time and MSG was the Mecca of college hoops.

In the 1946 tournament, URI faced Bowling Green University in the semifinals. Despite arriving in New York with a sparkling 19-2 record, URI was given little chance of winning. Dave Otten, Bowling Green's 6ft., 10 inch center, towered over Bob Shea, URI's tallest player at 6ft., 2 inches. The game was tight and hard-fought, but it gave birth to a Rhode Island legend in the person of URI point guard Ernie Calverly.

With the Rams down two points and time running out, Calverly, an All American who later played three years of professional basketball for the Providence Steamrollers, launched a 62 foot desperation shot (the distance was measured after the game) to tie the contest. URI won 82-79 in overtime. URI went on to face the mighty University of Kentucky and college basketball guru, Coach Adolph Rupp in the finals. URI lost the game by one point, but the age of racehorse basketball had begun.

The Calverly basket was christened as "The Shot Heard 'Round the World," and propelled him and URI into the upper stratosphere of college basketball. That same phrase was adopted in 1951 to describe New York Giant Bobby Thompson's epic winning home run in the third and deciding playoff battle with the Brooklyn Dodgers. (As a side note, native Rhode Islander Clem Labine hurled the Dodgers to a win to tie the series in game two the day before).

The URI win has an interesting post-script. No film evidence documents Calverly's miracle basket. Just before the shot, the game camera's film had run out and new film could not be loaded in time to capture Calverly's toss. Just image how many times that the shot would be replayed on ESPN or Fox Sports today.

Calverly went on to coach the University of Rhode Island basketball team for 11 seasons, compiling a 139-114 record, and guiding the team to two more NCAA tournaments. Calverly retired from URI in 1985 as the school's associate athletic director. He passed away on October 21, 2003 at the age of 79.

In the post-Calverly years, URI basketball has made its mark on the college hoops landscape with more NCAA appearances and wins, highlighted by the 2018 overtime victory over Big 12 opponent Oklahoma. The team also captured the Atlantic 10 regular season and tournament championships in 2018.

The Rams moved from Keaney Gym to the new 7,600-seat Ryan Center in 2002. In addition to Calverly, several URI players have gone on to pro basketball careers, including Claude English, Tom Garrick, Lamar Odom, and Cuttino Mobley. Former URI hoopster Al Skinner was at the helm of the Boston College Eagles for several years.

Today's URI players and coaches follow the trail of high speed basketball blazed by Frank Keaney and Ernie Calverly. No doubt, Keaney and Calverly are somewhere in the rafters of the Ryan Center rooting for the Runnin' Rams.

NOTE: *This column fulfills my promise to URI fans to write about the school's rich basketball history. Undoubtedly, they remember last month's column about the beginning of the Providence College basketball legacy. It also absolves my conscience as a URI graduate!*

COMPLAINT
DEPARTMENT

YOU CAN'T MAKE IT UP-CHAPTER I

Published April 2017, in *PrimeTime magazine*.

W e have all had a moment where astonishment eclipses reality, common sense becomes suspended, and you wonder about your command of the English language. In these brief, but baffling, exchanges with servers or sales clerks, you struggle to regain your sense of clarity. In that moment, remember the classic refrain, "You can't make this up."

Recently, I had one of those moments, so I decided to share a few of my favorites. Whether they happened to me or a friend, they really happened! The corporate names of these companies have been deleted to protect the guilty.

CHEAPER BY THE DOZEN: A friend told me of her experience in a popular donut shop. The shop offered a dozen donuts at half-price each afternoon after 2:00 p.m. While she was making her selections, the clerk declared that they had run out boxes that hold a dozen donuts, so she would use two half-dozen sized boxes. When my friend started to pay, the clerk charged her full price, curiously explaining that you had to buy a full dozen to get the discount. Luckily, the store manager intervened and solved this complex mathematical issue.

WATER, WATER EVERYWHERE: Another friend told me that she stopped into a well known fast food restaurant to buy three iced coffees. She had to take her medication, and asked for a cup of water. The teenage sentry, who was evidently in charge of cost reduction and crowd control, said no. The clerk explained that kids would ask for water and spray it all over the restaurant. My friend responded that she was 68 years old and assured her that she had no intention of creating mayhem. A plea to the manager was futile. (I would have left the coffee and demanded my money back).

CAN YOU HEAR ME NOW? I stopped at a local deli for a morning eye opener of a toasted cinnamon and raisin bagel with cream cheese on the side. After slowly and carefully placing my order, this conversation ensued:

Server: What kind of bagel do you want?
Me: Cinnamon raisin, please.
Server: Would you like that toasted?
Me: Yes, please.
Server: Would you like the cream cheese on the side or spread on
    the bagel?
Me: HRUMPH!

DRUGS OR PAPER PLEASE: I am an informal caregiver for my 80-year old, blind and disabled cousin who lives in subsidized housing. Each year, I gather her income and expenses for a summary necessary to complete her rent re-evaluation. I visited the local outlet of a large pharmacy chain to get this information. That's when the merry-go-round began to whirl.

When I requested the summary, I was questioned (rightfully so) if I was her legal power of attorney. I answered yes, but told them I did not have it with me. I offered to let them call my cousin to verify that I was her general and financial power of attorney and empower me to make the request on her behalf. The pharmacist refused.

I had picked up dozens of prescriptions for her at this same location, so I asked incredulously, "You will give me drugs but not a paper summary of her co-payments?" "Yes, he said." In frustration, I retorted "Doesn't that strike you as absurd"? Hah! I had stumped the corporate robot. He mumbled incoherently and could not explain his curious logic. He did, however, promise to send the summary to her "immediately." Immediately, as it turned out, required two additional phone calls and a two-week wait!

NEW MATH: As a grammar school student, I remember the drone-like repetition of addition and subtraction problems, multiplication tables, fractions and other methods of antiquity in the study of mathematics. Today, I am totally befuddled by the need to PROVE five times five equals 25. The following true life experiences PROVES that schools would serve the nation and the business world much better by teaching REAL NUMBERS rather than cluttering young minds with empirical studies of arithmetic.

ONE PLUS ONE IS STILL TWO: While shopping at the store of a well known grocery chain, I bought an item worth 98 cents. I gave the clerk $1.03 and she sternly informed me that I needed another nine cents to complete the transaction. In the interest of saving the world from mathematical illiteracy, we slowly re-enacted the sale and I got my nickel.

TRAINING DAY: I ordered a medium iced coffee at the local outlet of a national café. I became leery when the pleasant teen behind the counter asked ME how to ring up the order. Even though I helped her to find the iced coffee line on the menu board, she insisted on charging me for a latte. The iced coffee was price was $2.22 and she charged me $2.06. I gave her $2.11 and received 13 cents change. Obviously, she was a victim of new math training.

But, we're not quite finished yet. The young lady poured hot coffee into a cup and proudly announced she would garnish it with ice. Thankfully, a more experienced worker showed her where the iced coffee was apparently hidden.

THE BRITANNY SPEARS GEOGRAPHY PRIZE: I've saved the best for last. Brittany Spears once marveled that her talent enabled her to travel the world by declaring, "I get to go overseas to places like Canada."

Six years ago, my family and I were returning home from a week's vacation on North Carolina's Outer Banks. My daughter approached the first checkpoint at Dulles Airport with one-year old Nicholas in her arms. It was then that the TSA agent told her to return to the ticket counter for another boarding pass. When my daughter asked why, she was told, "You are going on an international flight." For the record we were flying to Liberty Airport in Newark, New Jersey! My daughter tried and failed to explain to the agent that Newark was in the state of New Jersey, but the line was growing longer.

Hearing this exchange (and petrified that this TSA staffer was partly responsible for my safety), I wanted to tell the agent that although we had been on vacation for a week, New Jersey had not ceded from the Union. Fearing a stint in airport jail for extreme sarcasm, I remained silent.

Miraculously, a TSA supervisor showed up and inquired about the log jam in the security line. When she heard the agent's reason, she sighed in amazement and calmly explained that Newark, New Jersey was actually IN the United States. The agent's reply was priceless, "Well I was never good at geography."

Take my advice. When your next Huh? moment comes, paste a smile on your befuddled face and repeat, "You can't make this up."

YOU CAN'T MAKE IT UP-CHAPTER II
Published January 2020, in PrimeTime magazine.

I n April 2017, I penned a *PrimeTime* column titled "You Can't Make It Up." It chronicled a few of my ordinary, daily encounters with corporate America, statewide government, and poorly trained "customer service" employees that left me utterly astounded and momentarily speechless! Welcome to "You Can't Make It Up-Chapter II."

The Creeping Driver Syndrome: If you're running late for an appointment. you CAN COUNT on being stuck behind a driver who thinks that 35 mph is just too fast for their Sunday driving habits. They are determined not to exceed the speed limit and crawl down the road at tortoise-like pace of 25. These are the same overly-cautious navigators that set a pace of 55 mph on the highway while driving in the fast lane. If you're en route to your annual physical and want your blood pressure and heart rate to approach normal, taking an alternate route is advisable.

The Parking Lot Blockade: While we are on the subject of vehicular courtesy (or lack thereof), you can always count on at least one rude or "entitled" driver to park his vehicle across two spaces. This absence of consideration is especially aggravating during the annual commercial feeding frenzy known as Christmas shopping.

The Gorilla Glued Folding Plastic Bag: We have all bought those rolls of plastic bags that need to be unfurled and unfolded before use. After considerable research and careful thought, I have concluded that the employees at bag manufacturing and packaging facilities surreptitiously smear a dab of super glue on some of the product before the cases are wheeled onto the loading dock to be trucked to your local stores. This diabolical plot inevitably leads to extreme frustration and a string of blue language that would make a sailor proud.

Child Proof Caps: We have all had to use a crowbar or vice grip to open those Child Proof prescription bottle caps. A more honest advisory should read, "Virtually Impossible to Open." The consumer would then be aware that determination, skill, and luck are required to access their medications.

Slippery and Tiny Medicine Bottle Safety Tabs: These alleged safety tabs covering the tops of your medication bottles are a first cousin to the Child Proof Caps. Pulling back these tiny, folded eel-slippery tabs to peel back the twice-glued cover requires fingers equipped with exceptionally gripping capabilities. Most of us finally resort to punching holes in the cap to avoid the inevitable frustration, permanent damage to our finger joints and scrapped knuckles.

The Mathematically Challenged Supermarket Customer: We have all encountered those "entitled" customers that are unable (or, more accurately unwilling) to count to 12 items or less to access the supermarket express check-out line. As a former grocery cashier who retired in 1969 at age 17 to attend college, I can tell you that the clerk is in a "no-win" situation. While they realize that the arithmetic scofflaw is trying the patience, courtesy, and good will of others in the express lane who CAN count, the cashier must adhere to the "Customer is Always Right" mantra.

The Time Challenged Physician: I am convinced that a doctor is required to discard ALL watches, clocks, and assorted time pieces when they earn their MDs. How else can you account for their lackadaisical approach to appointment times? One of my friends believes that he has solved this problem by calling ahead to the doctor's office to find out how far behind the physician's appointments are running behind so he can minimize his wait time. He reports very minimal success.

The Universal Robo Call: Recently, I had to change my telephone number. While I had to erase all memory traces of the number I had for 49 years from my memory bank, I was amazed to learn that my new exchange was an instant magnet for mysterious "800" numbers and calls from unfamiliar zip codes from the east, west, north, and south of the United States and other parts unknown. One such call "advised me that I would be arrested by the IRS for unpaid taxes and yet another threatened jail time over missed jury duty. (I've never been called to jury duty).

Still another call congratulated me on being the included in the will of Nigerian prince who had left me five million dollars. Good luck with that!

I'm sure you've all had your "You Can't Make It Up" moments in the past. No doubt that you will have many more in 2020. So remember to stay calm, breathe deeply, and retain your sense of humor!

TAKE MY TECHNOLOGY-PLEASE!!!

Published January 2019, in *PrimeTime magazine.*

The late comic Henny Youngman began each of his performances with the classic "Take my wife-please" opening line. While edgier observations would have defined my constant frustrations with modern technology, decorum and good taste have prevailed in headlining this column. Thanks, Henny.

My battles with online commerce and customer service are the legendary in my family. Every ticket order, technical question, and information request funneled through my computer requires a user ID, password, birthplace, name of my first pet, my first concert, favorite baseball team, and mother's maiden name. Stumbling to the end of these electronic interrogations, inevitably results in that dreaded red letter message declaring, "Your user ID or passwords don't match." Or maybe I forgot to include the last name of my father's fourth cousin in Albany. These infuriating technological insults always unleash a torrent of questionable language bouncing off the walls of my den.

For me, customer service is a personal transaction. I bristle at endless number prompts that transfer me to another robotic messenger. Risking arthritic index fingers, I push the "operator" button or repeat "representative" until I talk to a breathing human. The representative always advises me to go online to resolve my problem. I firmly advise that representative that I have waited an eternity to talk to a real person! (Spoiler alert: The corporate scions and bean counters want you to surrender and return to electronic hell).

Here are a few personal case histories documenting computer warfare.

Case One: Recently, my wife and I went to the airport to board a flight to the Caribbean for a six-day vacation. My wife believed that she had pre-registered us for the flight. At the airport, we were greeted by an airline employee who directed us to a kiosk. Despite our "pre-registration," the electronic gate agent demanded repetition of ALL of the information previously provided. We were instructed to print our own baggage tag, attach it to our luggage, and print our own boarding passes. The only task that any airline employee performed was weighing our luggage and heaving it on to the conveyor belt for the baggage handlers (robots perhaps?). In other words, I had become my own virtual gate agent. I wondered whether the "snacks and beverage service" on the flight would be dispensed from a vending machine.

Case Two: The Case One process reversed for our trip home.

Case Three: Last month, I purchased of tickets online to a Boston Bruins game. After enduring the inevitable user ID, password and registration gauntlet, the "tickets" showed up in my phone e-mail inbox. My son promptly deposited these "tickets" into my "virtual wallet." Being a natural skeptic, I decided to practice retrieving the "tickets" from my "cloud wallet." I failed the test. My twin granddaughters patiently explained to me the mysteries involved in retrieving these mythical ducats.

Case Four: Repeat Case Three, only this time for airline boarding passes for Philadelphia to return from vacation. No more than 30 seconds had elapsed before my virtual boarding pass vanished into electronic purgatory. While I was somehow to find it, my wife (who is much better with technology than I am) NEVER found hers. Fortunately, it was about 11:00 p.m. and a very compassionate gate agent allowed my wife to verify her identity using her passport.

Case Five: When we landed in Philadelphia, we had to pass through U.S. Customs and Immigration. It was time for another technology trial. The procedure is as follows:

You insert your passport into a kiosk and play 20 questions with the machine. If you answer all the questions correctly, the machine takes your picture (which resembles a mug shot taken at Alcatraz). You take your passport, customs and immigration forms and your prison photo to a REAL PERSON who conducts that final interview, stamps your forms, and green lights your re-entry.

Case Six: In Philadelphia, I bought a blueberry muffin while waiting for the final leg of our return trip to (SNOWY) Providence. I offered the cashier $3 in real U.S. currency for my purchase. I was handed a paper slip to insert into a scanner that charged the $3 to my CREDIT CARD! Even bakeries have succumbed to the technology age.

I offer two last case studies to illustrate my electronic skirmishes.

A few days ago, my e-mail address suddenly detached itself from the "cloud." My computer advised, "We are having trouble connecting to Google, but we will keep trying." After three days of waiting for "trying" to become success, I created a new e-mail address. Curiously, I can still access my previous electronic mailboxes using my phone.

The day after my e-mail obstruction issues were solved, one of my televisions decided to retire. Miraculously (for me), I traced the problem to a faulty converter box, got a new box from my cable provider, and installed it. You've probably guessed by now, reconnecting to television world did not go smoothly. I spent more than four hours in futile attempts to reprogram the remote control and re-establish the channel roster. Finally, I had to call a technician (I prefer magician) to get back on the "cloud's" broadcast route.

I believe that technology gods are sinister practical jokers who delight in my electronic misadventures. I can hear their boisterous laughter each time I plead, "Take My Technology-PLEASE!"

IRRITATION CAN BE INSPIRATIONAL

Published March 2020, in *PrimeTime magazine*.

Preparing for this column, I reached deeply into my literary closet, fished out my Curmudgeon Cap, and placed in firmly on my head. If imitation is the sincerest form of flattery, then irritation may be the best inspiration for columnists. As it's true for me, I'll share a few of my irritations turned inspirations with you.

I dislike restaurants featuring menus that contain more pages than *War and Peace*. I usually have an idea of what I want to order before setting foot in the dining room; but more choices lead to more time spent vacillating about my meal. Multiple options also tax my ability to relax and try the patience of the servers who dutifully await "my final answer." Then just when I believe I've made up my mind, they launch into a recital of the daily specials. Give me a menu printed on one sheet (two-sided at most), and I will be a very contented customer. It also helps to memorize your salad dressing preference beforehand, or be prepared to listen to a litany of choices.

The Theory of Limited Choices also works if I decide to have a beer before my meal. The elongated list of bottled, draft, or craft (particularly annoying in this new age of trendy suds) beer is aggravating and time consuming. Remember the Lum's Restaurant chain of the 1970s and 80s? Their marketing tag boasted about offering more than 50 kinds of beer. I don't think that there are any Lum's Restaurants still open. I suspect that the patrons spent too much time deciding on their beer, resulting in less table turnover and even lesser profits.

While we are on the subject of adult beverages, let's discuss vodkas. My wife Kathy sometimes orders a pre-dinner cocktail with the sophisticated-sounding "Cosmopolitan" handle. The server always reels off the roster of available vodkas, in ascending order of price, that are blended into a Cosmopolitan. Since she very seldom requests a specific brand, I suspect that her drink contains vodka just distilled from Idaho or Maine's most recent potato crop.

Moving away from eating and drinking diatribes, we now come to the inevitable aggravation associated with purchasing cell phones, home computers, and televisions. I AM, and my children, grandchildren, and friends agree, a communications dinosaur. In fact, I wear the label with pride and distinction. However, my analog-influenced hubris comes with a price.

Last month, we had to purchase a new television for our Florida condo. I approached the challenge with a considerable measure of unsettled terror. The salesperson regaled me with the features of steroid-enhanced HD, super HD, curved screen, and streaming capable "smart" televisions. In half-hearted jest, I asked where they hid the "stupid" sets. The process was complicated by the technical hurdle that required the television to be compatible with the newly acquired (but somehow strangely vintage) indoor antenna. I can report that Kathy and I miraculously managed to attach the antenna to the new "smart" television and trudge through the obstacle course of set-up options that scanned and saved the channels within our broadcast range (in digital, living color of course).

Currently, I glide blissfully across the mystical Cloud using my Version 6S cell phone. While the maker has now graduated to Version 11, I'm staying with Version 6S until I am ejected from the cell phone galaxy by ever-advancing technology and forced to buy an updated model. I understand that there are other types of cell phones. But given the limits of my technical acumen, I have no intention of straying from my current platform-whatever that means!

The same principles of aggravation, irritation, and dread apply when it comes to computers. My laptop is several years (and light years in generations) old. I write my columns, save my documents and correspondence, and keep many other types of records in a 7.0 Word program. In January, I received an ominous notification, warning, or veiled threat, that the manufacturer, "No longer supported the programs installed on my computer." I'm not really sure what that means, but it sounds serious! Am I a lapsed member of the digital age? Will the manufacturer's compliance officers knock down my door with a warrant and repossess my computer? Will I be hauled into Cloud Court and indicted for using an obsolete device? Only time will tell. Stay tuned. In the meantime, I will continue to convert my irritations into inspirations.

MUSINGS AND
MEMORIES

RELFECTING ON YEAR ONE
OF RETIREMENT

Published February 2016, in PrimeTime magazine.

I n what seems to be the blink of an eye, February marks Year One of my retirement. My first thoughts on reaching this milestone are reflected in the cliché-"Where did the time go?"

We had spent two years carefully preparing for our retirement . Our financial and legal houses were in order. We had decided to stay in our home. I had outlined the basic physical, social, emotional, and spiritual goals for my new life. Yet, as Departure Day of February 5 loomed ever closer, I faced the same questions and experienced the same emotions of many future retirees.

How would I manage the transition? How would we adjust to a new income pattern? Could I do all the things I wanted to do without over-scheduling myself? Even though Kathy had retired a year before me, I wondered if a new dynamic would emerge in our 45-year marriage. Above all, the biggest question was, "We had planned, but were we prepared?" Anticipation mixed with uncertainly creates an interesting emotional brew.

One year later, the report card is in and the marks are fantastic! The transition from the workforce to retirement has been smoother than I expected. I attribute this to the year of preparation and planning that eased the financial, emotional, and social impacts posed by a new life-style. For the most part, I have followed through with the guidelines I had sketched out in my mental "to do" list.

Our daily routine begins between 8:00 and 9:00 a.m. when Kathy and I have breakfast and read the newspaper. Before beginning the day in earnest, we have our "morning briefing." Kathy has her own volunteer work and social schedule, so she gives me the daily rundown on her plans for the day. I often joke with her that I'm going to buy a scheduling whiteboard from an office supply outlet where she can write her name and move the magnetic button to the "in" or "out" column!

Then I outline my day for her. At supper, we have the daily "de-briefing" the of comings, goings, issues, events, and "preview of coming attractions."

At least three times a week, I go to the gym for workouts on the treadmill and the stationary bike. Recently, I began taking guitar lessons a hiatus of more than 50 years. My limited repertoire now includes playing notes on four strings, strumming 10 chords, and picking several simple songs like Love Me Tender, Ode to Joy, and Tom Dooley. If I get stuck during practice, I call on the expertise of Sophia, my 12 year-old granddaughter, to help. She has been playing for two years and it much more advanced than I am.

I read or work on writing columns. Besides working a travel book based on our cross-country journey this spring, I am also outlining a cook book based on recipes developed by Kathy, Sophia, and her twin sister, Kailyn.

In addition to volunteering for the Senior Journal, a public access cable television program, I keep in touch with family, friends, colleagues, or re-connecting with others. For the last few years, I have helped my disabled 79 year-old cousin remain independent and living in her own apartment. I try to set aside a few "quiet moments" each day for rest and reflection. To be honest, I take an occasional afternoon nap or just listen to music.

We meet Sophia, Kailyn, and six year-old Nicholas at the bus stop two days a week and they hang out with us until my daughter or son-in-law to get home from work. Of course, there are the usual household errands and chores to be done, but now there is more time to do them. The day flies by and we are not bored. In fact, we understand the common question echoed by our retired friends, "How did we find the time to do all this when we were working?"

This summer, I met a friend in Narragansett and he gave me a refresher course in the art of quahogging, something I have not done in 55 years. While he harvested about two dozen quahogs, my efforts yielded a grand total of four. I guess my technique needs refinement. I will probably give it another try next summer, but I realized that it's simpler to buy prepared stuffed quahogs at the fish market! It's just not as much fun.

In addition to our cross-country trip, we joined friends this fall on a music mini tour to Memphis and Elvis country and to the seat of country music in Nashville. In July, our annual major league baseball tour stopped in St. Louis. We have been visiting major league ballparks with our sons and brothers-in-law since 1999. My sister-in-law Darlene will reveal her 2016 choice soon. Kathy and I took an anniversary trip to the Dominican Republic in November.

Tentative travel plans for 2016 include a family vacation with our children and grandchildren, six weeks in Florida, and the baseball trip. With any luck, I can fulfill a lifetime dream of visiting Tahiti.

We have been very fortunate. We have good health and the resources to live a productive and interesting retirement. As Frank Sinatra crooned, "It Was a Very Good Year," of adventures and experiences shaped by the opportunities of a new lifestyle. I can hardly wait for Year Two!

ALL JOBS GREAT AND SMALL

Published May 2016, in *PrimeTime magazine.*

W hen I tell people I've just met that I'm retired, they always ask "What kind of work did you do"? Automatically, I cite my career managing information and public relations programs for the Rhode Island Division of Elderly Affairs. Looking back, I realized that my 50-year work history included many jobs, great and small, beginning at age 11.

My first paying job was delivering the now-defunct *Providence Journal Evening Bulletin.* My 22-newspaper neighborhood route included homes, factories, jewelry shops, restaurants, and taverns. I was the distributor, customer service representative, and accountant for my small business.

In my early teens, I washed dishes at a six-table restaurant in downtown Providence. The pay wasn't great, but the food was delicious and was part of my daily compensation. About the same time, I worked as a janitor at my high school after classes as part of a federal Job Corp program popular during the early to mid 1960s.

At one time, I worked briefly in my cousin's exterminator business. It didn't take me long to realize that I wasn't cut out to crawl under houses in a reality version of a "Bug's Life," a rodent's life, or any other pest's life. The value of education became much clearer.

Just before my 16th birthday, I landed a job at the legendary Almacs supermarkets. For those not familiar with this historical and uniquely Rhode Island institution, you had to "know a guy" (and my parents did) to get a job. These jobs were coveted because you could eventually earn $2.65 per hour for part-time work, when many factory workers were making $1.65 per hour. You even got a paid vacation! For the next three years, I worked as a bagger, cashier, stocker, and produce clerk at Almacs stores from Providence to Kingston. The job helped to pay my tuition and expenses at URI. I left Almacs in my senior year at URI and held a string of part-time jobs that included bookbinding, packing frozen French fries, and more janitorial work.

One summer, my father hired me as a plater in the jewelry company where he was the foreman. Working in 100-plus degree heat and summer humidity, next to a row of tanks holding mysterious and foul-smelling chemical concoctions, preparing earrings, brooches, chains, etc. for a thin coating of gold solution was enough to convince me to stay in school. I'm sure that my father intended this job to be an object lesson! Later on, I operated an incinerator for the same company (pre-OSHA days).

I graduated from URI with a degree in Journalism in June of 1970 and was getting married that fall. Unable to find a position as a writer or reporter, I signed on as an order picker in an electrical supply warehouse of for a meager salary of $100 a week. A few months later, I jumped to the Adams Drug Company warehouse in Pawtucket for $110 a week. It wasn't a career move, but it was a $10 raise!

When Kathy and I returned from our honeymoon in November of 1970, I was offered a job as a quality control inspector for the Davol Rubber Company. The personnel manager was a friend of my wife's family. While I knew nothing about injection molding and rubber manufacturing, I finally began my writing career as editor and photographer of the *Davol Dialogue*, the company's house organ. I still have copies of the *Dialogue* in my personal "archives."

In 1974, I was hired as a technical writer for BIF. The company manufactured flow meters, pumps, valves and other technical equipment for power and waste water treatment plants. My friends and family thought my job title of technical writer was particularly amusing because I am technically-challenged. I can't figure out how to fold Flap A into Slot B. In addition to writing brochures and specification sheets, however, I took over as editor for their house organ, the *BIF Reporter*. We were far ahead of the coming communications trends when we produced the state's first video employee news program.

After being laid off from BIF in 1975, I began state service as a customer information specialist at the Rhode Island Division of Taxation under a yet another federal job training program. In the interest of full disclosure and in true Rhode Island style, my uncle was the state tax administrator at the time. Eventually, I became a revenue agent (yeah, one of those guys who goes out on the road and collects tax money). That position taught me the value of honest dialogue and business relationships, gave me stories that will last a lifetime, and provided fantastic insight into human nature. I also served as a media consultant for a Woonsocket town council candidate. He served two terms on the town council, but later lost a mayoral election.

In 1986, after 11 years in the Tax Division, I was hired as an information and public relations specialist for the Rhode Island Division of Elderly Affairs. For the next 27 years, I wrote and edited guide books, brochures, fact sheets and other materials designed to help seniors maintain their independence and dignity and help families identify programs to support their elder parents and relatives. With the help of many volunteers, we produced a nationally acclaimed public access cable television program focusing on the issues of growing older in Rhode Island.

On the sporting side, I was the coach for North Providence's Centredale boys and girls middle school basketball teams from 1995 through 2000.

Next time someone asks you what you do for a living, remember all those jobs you had along the way, great and small. Each one is a patch in the quilt of your personal history.

WHAT EVER HAPPENED TO 50 YEARS?

Published September 2016, in *PrimeTime magazine*.

"Time passes over us, but leaves its shadow behind."
-Nathaniel Hawthorne

The first hint that five decades had passed came in a "Save the Date" e-mail heralding the 50th reunion of my 1966 Classical High School graduating class. What? Wasn't it just last year I went to the 40th reunion? A few weeks later, I was mystically transported back to 1966 listening to the smooth harmonies of the Beach Boys at their 50th anniversary concert. It was true. Fifty years had somehow elapsed.

September and Labor Day always ushered in the start of a new school year and 1966 was going to be something special. Graduation would bring freedom from the regimen of daily quizzes. Latin, Greek mythology woven through the The Iliad and The Odyssey classics, algebra (which I still do not understand), chemistry, book reports, Hamlet, and Alan Poe's Raven would become distant memories. There were dances, football and Friday night basketball games for the Purple, as we were known, to see and to be seen. College, the first taste of life away from home, and untold new adventures loomed on the horizon.

In 1966, Classical High School was a gothic yellow (yes, yellow) brick building situated just behind the current school. The windows emitted ghostly groans when they were pried open. The study hall was a cavernous auditorium that seemed to echo every whisper and magnify the sound of every dropped pencil. The well worn wooden floor boards showed the wear and tear of a few hundred thousand shoes (yes, shoes, not sneakers). The ancient stairways clanked with each step.

To understand a memory excursion spanning 50 years, a frame of reference is required. In 1966, the closing Dow Jones average was 785. The cost of a new sedan was about $2,650 and you could fill it with gas at 32 cents a gallon. The median income was $6,900 and you could buy a new house for $14,200.

Much to the delight of teenage boys, mini-skirts were in vogue. Indira Gandhi was elected prime minister of India and Lyndon B. Johnson was the president of the United States, having been sworn in on Air Force One after the assassination of John F. Kennedy in Dallas, Texas in 1963.

Hit movies included Doctor Zhivago and the James Bond thriller Thunderball. The Monkees, Beatles, Rolling Stones, and the Mamas and the Papas joined the Beach Boys in ruling the radio bands. Popular television shows included Bonanza, the Beverly Hillbillies, the Lucy Show, and Bewitched. The Ed Sullivan Show, where the Beatles were introduced to America in February 1964, was a Sunday evening tradition.

The NFL Green Bay Packers trounced the AFL Kansas City Chiefs 35 to 10 in Super Bowl I, held in the Los Angeles Coliseum. The Baltimore Orioles swept the Los Angeles Dodgers, who moved from Brooklyn in 1958, four games to none on the 1966 World Series. I think that made many jilted Brooklynites happy.

In 1966, the nation was in the midst of a political, cultural, and social revolution. The drums of protest against the Viet Nam War were rumbling ever louder by the day. The civil rights movement, punctuated by riots in many city streets and loud cries of injustice in the halls of Congress, lurched toward equality for African Americans. The Civil Rights and Voting Rights Acts, and Medicare were now the law of the land.

The button-down, conservative norms of corporate America were challenged by a younger generation of workers demanding careers that did not fit traditional employment models. Social mores were tossed around like beach balls in the wind. Centuries old religious dogmas and traditions were being questioned. It was the era of sex, drugs, and rock and roll. A Chinese proverb states, "May you live in interesting times." The 1960s were more than interesting. They were a seismic shift American history.

Since graduating from Classical, life, as the saying goes, has happened. I graduated from URI in 1970. I have been married to Kathy, a remarkable woman, for almost 46 years. We have savored and appreciated the good times and weathered the challenging times together. We have traveled through Italy, Ireland, and the Caribbean. Since retiring, we have shared a cross-country drive and a winter in Florida. With any luck, trips to France, Monaco, and Tahiti are in our future.

Our daughter, Kate and her husband, Ray live in North Providence with our 13-year old twin granddaughters Kailyn and Sophia (Kailyn always asks to be listed first because she is one minute older than Sophia), and six-year old Nicholas. Our son Matthew has lived and worked in Las Vegas for 13 years and Benjamin lives in Manhattan and works in New Jersey.

The lessons of preparation, solid study habits, and discipline learned at Classical High School have served me well in my life and career. After the daily demands of Classical academic requirements, college seemed much easier. The older I became, the more I appreciated the life lessons I learned at Classical.

When I read the announcement of my 50th high school reunion, I decided to not alter the images of my youth with the realities of senior citizenship. But the opportunity to see old classmates, wander the halls of Classical High and sit at its petrified wooden desks once again in virtual reality changed my mind. The reunion will connect past to the present, and lend new perspective to the future.

As I researched this column, I came across a quote by Marty Rubin observing, "Time does not pass, it continues." How true.

BEWARE THE IDES OF MARCH

Published March 2017, in PrimeTime magazine.

With my granddaughters Kailyn and Sophia preparing to enter high school next year, I began to recall my literary, Latin, and ancient history training at Classical High School in Providence. Since it's March, a warning to Julius Caesar in Shakespeare's play of the same name is permanently embedded in the corners of my mind, "Beware the Ides of March." History records that Caesar, Emperor of Rome, ignored the advice of his soothsayer and went to the Roman Forum. He was stabbed to death by Roman Senators on March 15, the Ides of March. Even his former friend and close ally Brutus was a member of the attacking cohort. Caesar's last were allegedly, "Et Tu Brute?" (And you too Brutus)?

What does that have to do with my granddaughters? As I thought about the Ides of March, I wondered if school still taught the Classics. Although it was painful and seemed irrelevant at the time, we were required to study Latin For at least two years. While I didn't realize it while I was struggling to translate Caesar's war chronicles "Gaul is divided onto three parts" from Latin to English, the plain fact is that Latin provided me with a solid foundation in Romance languages and the root of words that can be traced to their Latin origins. This training has become an invaluable asset in my 40-year career as a trained professional writer.

Going down the Latin memory lane triggered echoes of the regimen of many other high school courses. For example, required reading included Homer's epic Greek Iliad and Odyssey. While both were difficult to understand, they opened our eyes to the mythology of 683 Greek gods and the divine powers of such luminaries as Achilles, Poseidon, Zeus, Athena, or Ulysses. Studying Greek classics is a great way to stimulate the imagination. I doubt that any ancient Greek literature is included in today's high school curriculum. I believe that the students are the losers in this educational omission.

So now we come to American literary classics. Does anyone read 1984 by George Orwell, The Grapes of Wrath by John Steinbeck, or The Raven by Edgar Allan Poe? American literature is rich in cultural, historical, and societal treasures. Such masterpieces are meant to be read and enjoyed.

There is one particular memory of high school subjects still sends chills up my spine-Algebra! I confess that it took me two years to master Algebra I. This mathematical enigma was as baffling to me as Egyptian hieroglyphics. If the truth be told, I still believe that my teacher passed me on the second try because she KNEW that I was never going to grasp Algebra. Undoubtedly, she wanted to spare me the embarrassment of being a junior in a freshman math class. Despite her contention that I would use Algebra in my everyday life, I remained, and still remain, unconvinced. Fortunately, Kailyn and Sophia have taken pre-Algebra math in junior high school. It's my sincere hope that they did not inherit my mathematical deficiencies.

To their advantage, my granddaughters have been given a solid foundation in history, science, math, music, the performing arts and other academic disciplines in their current school system. Each month, they are assigned to work in groups on a specific class project. This exercise teaches them the principles of planning, teamwork, responsibility, accountability, and presentation skills. They will need all of these skills as they move along in their educational journey.

Maybe they won't read about Greek mythology or the conquests of Julius Caesar. But you can be sure that their own Ides of March warning will arrive when the schedule for mid-term exams is announced.

HURRICANE CAROL REVISITED

Published August 2018, in PrimeTime magazine.

One of the most devastating hurricanes to make landfall in Rhode Island began as a tropical disturbance in the Bahamas. By the time Hurricane Carol slammed into the Ocean State on August 25, 1954, it had torn up the southern New England coastline leaving more than 60 persons dead and hundreds of millions of dollars in property destruction in its wake. To those people who were old enough, Carol brought back memories of the unnamed hurricane of 1938.

The coastal communities of Newport, Westerly, Warwick, and the Edgewood section of Cranston and Providence faced the brunt of Carol's wrath. By the time Carol finally left the battered state, 19 people had perished; 4,000 homes were obliterated or washed out to sea; 90 million in damage had been wrought; 200 boats were smashed into timber; and downtown Providence was submerged under 12 feet of flood waters. Some reports pegged Carol's maximum wind speed at 125 mph. On Block Island, the wind speed was clocked at an astounding 135 mph. The power and impact of Carol was so impressive that the name was removed from the national hurricane roster for 10 years!

My recollections of August 25 are anchored in the powerful images of nature's fury as seen through the eyes of a five year old, my age in 1954. My grandfather owned a small one-room beach shack in the Conimicut Beach section of Warwick. I slept on a cot (I guess) on the small screened in front porch when we stayed with my grandfather. Shortly after school let out for the summer, many families who, were related to each other one way or another, packed up their belongings and moved from living next to each other on Crary Street in South Providence to almost-next to each other in what de facto became Crary Street South in Conimicut.

Earlier that summer, we had stopped at the local hardware store in Conimicut to buy streamers for handgrips on my bicycle. I spent many glorious summer hours pedaling up and down the street fast enough to make the streamers fly in the wind! On weekends, my father and uncles would drive "down the beach" to dig for quahogs. What they did not eat right there on the spot would be put into the red gravy for the spaghetti and quahog feast that night.

That was all before August 25, 1954. I recall sitting on my grandfather's porch that morning and seeing an ominous, angry dark sky. While we would have frequent short rain showers during the summer, these threatening clouds were buffeted by very strong winds. The tall, slender tree in the small front yard was nearly bent in two. Looking towards another section of Conimicut cove, I saw walls of brown water raging over the beach and just beginning to spill on to the road.

Not too long after (a five year-old kid's memory of time has certain gaps), my father drove to the beach to take my mother, my one-year old sister, and my grandfather home and out of harm's way. My grandfather refused to leave. The reason was much more financially motivated than sentimental. True to many of his generation who distrusted banks after the Great Depression, they kept their money with them and hide it in curious places. During the winter, he kept it in the freezer and hidden in several places around his house. In the summer, he carted it to the beach house and stored it in a locked cast iron stove in a shed.

While I don't remember the words in the obviously testy exchange between my father and grandfather, my father's ultimatum was perfectly clear. He would take his family home and if my grandfather wanted to stay and perish with his money, he could. While my grandfather did choose to leave with us, I remember watching him struggle against powerful winds to retrieve his "fortune."

Many days after the hurricane, when we were allowed to return to the site of shack to assess the damage Carol had caused. Astonishment quickly overwhelmed curiosity. Nothing was left. Not a shingle, not a window, not a wall, no clothing, no appliances, and certainly not that cast iron stove/safe. Carol, the giant eraser, had obliterated the shack and any traces of time spent there. Ironically, 63 years later, that small plot of land is still unoccupied. It stands as a ghostly reminder of lost summers.

On August 31, 1954, the *Providence Journal* published "Hurricane Carol Lashes Rhode Island." This impressive collection of photos and news stories from August 25 and the aftermath gives the reader some insight as to the fury of the storm. From time to time, I re-read my faded copy. Copies are available on line.

Every year when the names of the potential hurricanes are announced, my memory re-plays the vivid images of nature's raw power unfold before his eyes. I see my grandfather battling wind and rain to get to his money and think of the adage, "A fool and his money are soon parted." In his case, it would have read, "A fool and his money were soon departed."

I suppose that many of us who survived August 25, 1954 have measured other hurricanes to Carol when comparing the devastation, property loss, and human loss that each storm imposes on our community. As seen through the eyes of a five-year-old, such comparisons are meaningless because they diminish the terrifying impact of what was seen that day, first hand.

NOTE: *Hurricane Carol Revisited, April 2016: When my sister, Maryann, read this column, she pointed out one detail that I had missed. I had forgotten that the Infant of Prague statue was the only thing left standing as Hurricane Carol swept our beach cottage out to sea. My mother used to light a candle and place it in the candle holder as a plea for special intentions.*

THE GREAT BLACKOUT BLUES-GIVE OR TAKE 53 YEARS

Published January 2018, in PrimeTime magazine.

As evening loomed on Tuesday, November 9, 1965, I settled down at my desk in our South Providence second floor tenement to study for Wednesday's battery of Classical High School quizzes. Daily tests in each subject were standard in our demanding curriculum.

At precisely 5:16 p.m., the lights flickered and went out. Like many tenements of the era, the electricity flowed through old fashioned fuses. My father went into the basement to replace what he assumed was a blown fuse. He quickly discovered that none of the fuses had flamed out. Later, we learned that we were one of 30 million people who lost power in the Great Blackout of 1965.

A tripped 230-kilowatt transmission line in Ontario, Canada, had plunged the provinces of Ontario and parts of Quebec, all of the New England states and part of New York into sudden darkness. The blackout had triggered massive rush hour traffic delays, trapped thousands of persons in elevators, and froze the New York City subway system with more than 800,000 jammed in crowded cars.

For all the commotion the Great Blackout of 1967 caused, I have fond memories of the power outage. After all, Wednesday's quizzes were cancelled! The reprieve was temporary because electricity was restored on a rolling basis over the next 24 hours. Regular daily testing resumed on Thursday. Many a Classical student hoped that the blackout persisted, at least through the semester exam period.

Fast forward to sometime between the evening of October 29 and the morning of October 30 this year. Matthew, a powerful storm with wind speeds and gusts well over 74 miles per hour (the marker for promoting a tropical storm to a hurricane) knocked out electricity to more than 1.3 million customers across New England and other Northeast locations. In Rhode Island, approximately 145,000 were without power.

We had previously experienced periodic power failures whenever of the house's circuit breakers were tripped. So I thought that the blinking digital bedroom clock signaled one of those interruptions at some point during the night. It wasn't long before I found out that the massive storm had cut power to wide swaths of the east coast. It took several days to restore the power to all Rhode Islanders. We were without electricity for about 36 hours. It was an interesting 36 hours.

During the power outage, we listened to news and music on our battery powered radio. It didn't take long to realize how much time we typically spent watching television, especially since there was no television to watch! I never realized how many times I walked into a room and automatically flipped the light switch. During those powerless 36 hours, I repeated that reflex action countless times, only to be greeted by darkness. Not only that, but cell phone service went silent!

The daylight hours did not pose much of an inconvenience. Our main task was to limit the times we opened the refrigerator. We had to be even more judicious in opening the freezer. It remained closed for most of the blackout.

My wife and I passed the time that evening playing cards and talking by the light of candles strategically located around the dining room. The "down time" was actually quite relaxing. But unlike 1965, when I was longed for a longer power failure to delay the inevitable daily testing routine, I wanted the electricity to be restored quickly. How times do change.

Coincidentally, we were also affected this summer by a blackout that occurred 700 miles away. We had booked a beach house for a family vacation in August at Cape Hatteras, North Carolina. We were looking forward to spending time with our son Ben and his new wife, Renee, my daughter Kate, son-in-law Ray, and grandchildren Kailyn, Sophia, and Nicholas. We drove to my sister in law's home in Virginia two days before the vacation was to start to break up the 18-hour journey south. In Virginia, we began to see news reports revealing that all three power transmission lines to the island had been severed. A worker had accidently sliced through the electric cables during construction of a new bridge. The island was in the dark.

The lower end of Cape Hatteras where we were headed was being evacuated and access was limited to residents. Power restoration efforts varied from three days up to three months, depending on the reporting source. After three days of waiting, it was apparent that the Hatteras vacation would be cancelled. As an alternate plan, we decided to spend two days in Virginia Beach as a "consolation prize." Seven-year old Nicholas was quick to point out his disappointment because, as he declared, we had promised him a week at the beach. Despite his objections, we enjoyed our family time together...in the sunlight!

Maybe this year, power outages and blackouts will be just memories.

HOW TERRIBLY STRANGE TO BE (AL-MOST) 70 (WITH APOLOGIES TO SIMON AND GARFUNKEL)

Published February 2018, in *PrimeTime magazine.*

Okay. Okay. I'm taking literary license, with an appropriate nod to sudden thoughts. I will celebrate my 69th birthday on February 21, but it marks the beginning of my 70th year. So the story begins here.

While listening to a Simon and Garfunkel collection driving home from Cape Cod recently, a spontaneous inventory of life experiences was triggered by the track, "Old Friends." Whimsically tucked into the musical conversation of this mystical song were the lyrics, "Can you image us years from today, sharing a park bench quietly? How terribly strange to be 70." Terribly strange indeed!

Since both of my parents had passed away by the time they were 65, I had no personal frame of reference to rely on as a guide for growing older. When I look at photos of them in their late 50s and early 60s, they seemed to have aged beyond their years. I believe that their physical appearance was not so much a consequence of advanced age, but a sign of a being worn down by a much more demanding life.

Building a personal life history is simultaneously challenging, intriguing, frustrating, rewarding, and revealing. A look at the good, the bad, and the ugly is a reflective trip down memory lane and can be a road map to the future. Even regrets can lead the way to a more peaceful life if you look for the insights they provide. My regrets are few.

I am grateful for the many gifts I have been blessed with during my life. My parents inspired in me a desire to pursue an education. Like most working class parents of their generation, they wanted their children to escape the drudgery of factory work.

The sight of my father slowly climbing the stairs to our second floor tenement after spending a day in the sweltering and oppressive plating room his factory made a lasting impression on me. One summer he arranged a job for me in that very department. His "object lesson" was not lost on me. This lesson, and so many others subtly taught, inspired (or maybe frightened me) to complete my education. I became a professional writer, earned enough to move from a rented home in South Providence to a home my wife and I owned and eventually paid off, raised our children, and retired with a degree of financial security, an ability to travel, and enjoy life.

I have been married to my best friend, confidant, co-worker in child rearing, life coach, companion, fiscal and budgetary director, (and impartial literary critic) Kathy for more than 47 years. The good times were easy, but enduring the rough times, as well as physical and emotional challenges has given us a profound appreciation for a life spent together.

Our children have learned independence with individuality, hard work and generosity, compassion, faith, love, and laughter. (Nobody has moved home yet!) Our twin teenage granddaughters and eight-year-old Nicholas will be joined by a new grandson in August. We look forward to creating more memories with our growing family.

Most of our working years were spent in careers that were interesting, creative, and fulfilling. When the time came to retire a few years ago, we left our jobs enriched by the experiences we had and the people we met. Our transition to a life without employment was easier than we had anticipated.

Retirement has enabled us to drive cross-country, a personal Great American Road Trip, travel to Paris and the French countryside, escape New England winters by migrating to Florida, and co-author two books. If the past is indeed prologue, there are more adventures in our future.

Common to all recollections are tinges of nostalgia. The age of digital communications has dulled the skills required for true interpersonal exchanges. An e-mail (or the impersonal, dreaded e-vite) has none of the warmth or emotion of a note. I don't feel the aura of personal contact. The art of handwriting a letter is lost and electronic messages often contain hieroglyphic symbols and corrupted words that make it difficult or even impossible for me to decipher. (Maybe that's the point). In many cases, people choose to hide behind computer generated message, relayed via the amorphous "cloud," rather than invest in an actual conversation. How unfortunate.

Appliances and other gadgets did not require a degree in engineering to assemble or repair. Cars were not mobile computers. You could actually talk to a customer service representative on the telephone without enduring the endless routine of prompts delivered by a robot. Dinners were seasoned with conversations that were not interrupted by endless checking of largely superfluous e-mails and updates on mundane daily routines. The pace of life was slower, but interactions were more meaningful.

I've come to believe that it's NOT terribly strange to be 70. (Sorry boys). It's just another numbered mythical "milestone" in the arithmetic of personal history. Maybe the real answer to successful aging (however you define success) is captured in this amazingly simple lyric in the James Taylor song, "The Secret O' Life," when he sings, "The secret of life is enjoying the passage of time."

Sound advice or wishful thinking? You decide for yourself.

A COLUMN ABOUT COLUMNS

Published July 2018, in PrimeTime magazine.

In a few hours, this blank computer screen will be transformed into a column that will make its way onto the pages of this month's *PrimeTime* magazine. After sending it off by "cloud." I'll take a brief "time out," and begin planning next month's essay.

From time to time, friends and family members ask me where I get the ideas for columns, how the ideas, inspirations, or memories somehow get translated to words, and why do I continue to write. The why is perhaps the easiest question to answer.

I spent nearly 40 years of my career writing for private corporations, political campaigns, and state agencies and using the journalistic skills I learned at the University of Rhode Island. As with many URI School of Journalism graduates in the late 1960s and the 1970s, I was trained and mentored by the demanding guiding hand of legendary *Providence Journal* reporter turned college instructor, the late Wilbur Doctor. He instilled in all of us an appreciation for getting the facts correct and writing a simple, understandable story in an economy of words, using correct spelling, grammar, and syntax. While our efforts were returned with his blunt criticisms, Doctor always added words of encouragement to his comments. These lessons have served me well and I still use them as a columnist. In most columns, I choose to add generous dashes of humor to the creative mix. I write for enjoyment and to exercise my aging brain…mostly for the enjoyment.

Topics for columns are derived from a variety of sources. The column about Rhode Island pirate Thomas Tews was sparked by visits to the Outer Banks in North Carolina and a Key West afternoon spent in a museum looking over buried treasure unearthed off the shores of Florida, the Caribbean, and other tropical waters. The column about lesser known entertainers was developed after watching an old black and white television program. Still others are the result of simple twists, turns, and extraordinary ironies of everyday ordinary life. In other words, topic ideas can come from anywhere if I keep my literary antennae up.

You may be surprised to learn that depending on what is churning in my moderately creative mind, I may start by writing a prospective title. I may write the end of the column first, or the middle, or even the first paragraph. When it comes to writing a column, my stating rule is to have no rule, trust your instincts, and listen to your inspirations.

After my initial thoughts are written, I begin listing the elements I want to appear in the column, conduct required factual research and references, and verify any quotes or other material that will become part of the finished product. These elements for the column are scribbled in a notebook in no particular order. In the interest of accuracy, "scribbled" is all too true. The Sisters of Mercy would be horrified to learn that years of Palmer Method penmanship have become a distant memory. It's hard to believe that this collection of English hieroglyphics will eventually morph into a fairly cohesive essay. By some cosmic force, the column always seems to materialize.

Next, I create an outline that will be the roadmap for the first draft. This process will put the pieces of the jigsaw note puzzle into a complete, if imperfect, picture. When the first draft is finished, it's proofread to correct spelling and grammar mistakes. As you have probably guessed by now, I have temporarily exhausted my creative juices and put the column aside for the day. This literary "exhaustion" often leads to a nap.

The next day, I read the draft with fresh eyes and look for any additional corrections, check the column for factual errors, logical order of paragraphs, narrative tightness and cohesiveness, and any other glaring missteps before editing the draft. After the second draft is completed, the column undergoes a rigorous review from the in-house editor, my wife Kathy. Despite my writing, reading and re-reading the column, my mind's eye sees what I intended to write, but might not actually appear on the page. For this reason, her input is vital.

After the column has been reviewed and critiqued, the final edits are made. After a final reading for any last minute changes, the column is finished and ready to be sent off! I don't "over-read" the column because I want to preserve its freshness, flavor, and humor. I don't know if this "system" will work for other writers, but it seems to work for me.

I've saved this question for last. Sometimes I'm asked how much I get paid for writing this column. Sorry, I plead the Fifth… it's a trade secret. Let's just say my reward and sense of accomplishment is in the column's creation, not the remuneration.

ARE NEWSPAPERS THE
NEXT MEDIA DINOSAURS?

Published October 2018, in PrimeTime magazine.

Recently, I read an obituary for the Pittsburgh Post Gazette. The last printed version of this daily newspaper hit the streets on August 28, marking the death of a publication that can trace its roots to its first edition on July 29, 1786. For anyone keeping score, the Post Gazette made it to the ripe old age of 232 years and one month. The paper will continue to exist in its web format.

For a former Providence Journal Bulletin delivery boy, the now silent presses of the Post-Gazette lend weight to what many media experts are predicting...the demise of the printed newspaper. Future generations may one day refer to print edition newspapers as media dinosaurs. When and if that day comes, we will all be the lesser for it.

The concerns of many journalists and avid newspaper readers are not unfounded. In 1970, more than 1,700 daily newspapers were published in the United States. In 2017, less than 1,300 remained. Readership studies also show that from 2004 to 2012, daily newspaper readership dropped from 54 percent to 38 percent! Some surveys pegged that rate at 29 percent in 2017.

If you doubt the demise of print media, the Providence Journal provides daily testament to the "modernizing" (that's what media conglomerates call purchasing a local newspaper, laying-off or buying out seasoned reporters and columnists, taking a scalpel to community news space, and filling the pages with wire reports) of statewide daily editions. Regional news bureaus are extinct and a significant amount of city and town news is squeezed into brief summary columns on page two.

For additional evidence, pick up what late Mayor and radio personality Buddy Cianci called the Providence Pamphlet. Monday Journal editions affirm that his observation was more fact than fiction. The

Providence Sunday Journal is but a slimmed-down shadow of its predecessors.

In my opinion, the Providence Journal has abandoned its local roots and gutted its once talented staff of local news and sports reporters and columnists for homogenized content with diluted connections to its Rhode Island heritage. Profit now reigns over information, education, and community responsibilities. Despite these drawbacks, daily newspaper reading remains a staple of my morning routine.

There are a myriad of reasons for the slow, inexorable decline of the printed daily newspaper. Equipment, newsprint, and staff are expensive. The number of pages in any edition of a newspaper can be proportional to advertising money generated and fees collected by publishing legal notices, obituaries, etc. Considerable chunks of advertising budgets are now directed to other media platforms and newspapers are perpetually engaged in a tug of war for those same funds.

Perhaps the most significant factor in declining printed newspaper consumption is the explosion of Internet and social media sites that deliver the events of the day in nanosecond time frames and sound bites. For better or for worse (and I consider it worst), many people gather their "news" from websites that give them what they have come to expect...the world in 30 seconds or less. In many instances, scanning headlines has replaced reading the actual news stories.

To be sure, many sites offer opinions, disguised as "news," tinted by their own perspectives. But the implications of this "now and fast" consumption deprives us of the background, context, texture, and meaning of the stories. Sadly, these missing elements are precisely what involved, informed, and concerned people need to make intelligent decisions about issues and political candidates. The variety of perspectives is valuable only when we take the time to read and analyze them. It's the time worn axiom, "You can lead a horse to water" principle.

As a corollary to this theory, continued attacks on the legitimacy and intent of a free press have a chilling effect on one of the most vital underpinnings of our system of governance. A free press was envisioned by the founding fathers as a checkpoint against partisan majority rule or totalitarian government. The news media is not, nor was it ever intended to be, a cheerleader for any political leader or party. These basic principles are being dangerously battered, bludgeoned, and maligned on a daily basis.

So in a way, I guess, this column is a variation of the bumper sticker that reads, "Support your local sheriff." Think of it as a "Support your community daily newspaper" commercial. The time you spend reading the paper will expand your knowledge base and give you a wider perspective on current events and issues. The results are not only tangible, but also necessary to preserving our freedoms and exercising the right to vote responsibly and effectively.

And also save the daily newspaper from media extinction.

NOTE: *The Providence (Rhode Island) Journal, the state's largest daily newspaper began publishing in 1829. It is the oldest continuously published daily news paper in the United States (Wikipedia). The Providence Journal once boasted a daily circulation of approximately 200,000. In March 2020, GateHouse Media, the parent company of the paper, reported a daily circulation of 41,000.*

ON THE FLY: MUSINGS OF A FULL-FLEDGED SNOWBIRD

Published April 2019, in *PrimeTime magazine.*

Since leaving Rhode Island on January 1, Kathy and I have escaped (hopefully) howling winter wind gusts, arctic blasts, snow, sleet, slush, and other assorted winter weather offerings.

Having spent more than three months in Ft. Lauderdale, Florida we've officially accepted the title of "Snowbird."

Some of the differences between a New England winter and winter here in southern Florida are obvious, others are more subtle. Obviously, my daily wardrobes require less layers of clothing. The standard uniform includes shorts, T-shirt, and sandals. Occasionally, I "dress up" with a collared polo shirt for a night out. Since arriving here on January 3, I've worn long pants and socks less than a half dozen times and my sweatshirt has been fished out of the closet only twice.

We spend much of our time outdoors. The village of Lauderdale-By-The-Sea is very close to our apartment. In four-block square, you can walk the village and eat at restaurants offering a wide variety of menus, duck into everything-you-could-want stores, pet shops (more about them later), and ice cream parlors (my favorite stops). The restaurants feature happy hours from either 3:00 or 4:00 p.m. until 7:00 p.m. Drinks and appetizers are half price and all eateries feature continuous live music. On weekends, the square is blocked off. That's your signal to relax in a plaza beach chair and listen to bands playing anything from hard rock to 80s and 90s popular music. If you prefer a more boisterous, busier environment, the beachfront at Ft. Lauderdale would fit the bill.

There are no fees for public beaches along the Deerfield, Pompano, and Ft. Lauderdale shoreline, but parking lots are metered and you pay an hourly rate for your sun worshipping. On average, you will spend $5 for three hours of beach time.

The pace of life in south Florida is much slower. It does take time adjusting to a more relaxed lifestyle; but not as long as you would think. I pass the days reading, playing golf (my game has NOT improved), at the pool, or walking the beach. Wintering here has re-charged my batteries. When we get home, we will be ready to resume our "northern" routine that includes doctor and dentist appointments, grandchildren transportation services, attending school functions, watching baseball and softball games, and spending time with our family and friends.

Those are the obvious differences. The more subtle aspects of life and times in southern Florida might surprise you.

While New Jersey could stake a legitimate claim as the Diner Capital of the Universe, Ft. Lauderdale can proclaim itself as the Strip Mall Capital of the World. Almost every commercial block is home to mini shopping plazas. It seems that each strip mall houses a medical clinic; doctors office; optometrist; chiropractor; dermatologist; dentist; lawyer; traffic violation fixer; real estate agent; restaurant; pet groomer and supply store; convenience store; pawn shop; furniture outlet; consignment store; check cashing site; psychic; smoke and Vape shop; nutrition and vitamin emporium; wellness, massage, and nail spa; and tax preparer.

On the automotive front, many cross-town thoroughfares are pit stops for dealerships showcasing exotic car brands such as Jaguar, Maserati, Rolls Royce, Bentley, Lamborghini, Ferrari, Mercedes, muscle car Mustangs, Chargers, Corvettes, and other pricey rides.

Speaking of cars, driving in south Florida requires intense concentration, patience, skill, anticipation, alertness, and pure luck. Danger lurks on almost every main street because each road is the reincarnation of Mineral Spring Avenue on steroids (or as our pastor Father John calls it, Miserable Spring Avenue).

Most main roads in Ft. Lauderdale are at least three or four lanes wide. Turn signals appear to be disabled and horns could well be set on permanent BLARE mode. If you have the patience to wait out the interminable light changes and the phenomenon of legal turns on green arrows (imagine that scenario in Rhode Island), you will be "urged" to accelerate on a green light, with all haste, by a horn blast issued at the one half-second mark. At the other end of the spectrum, traffic flows often devolve suddenly into a five-lane, 20 mph crawl fest.

On the highways, cars make three or four lane change maneuvers (without directional signals) at a terrifying rate. Apparently, Florida street jockeys studied at the Daytona 500 School of Driving. It's also necessary to know your destination route BEFORE you embark on a south Florida turnpike experience. Lanes merge quickly and you could find yourself in an "Exit Only" lane in an instant. That miscalculation can be nerve rattling. Florida drivers believe that they were endowed with inalienable pass-on-the-right, traffic-line-be-dammed privileges when they attained their licenses. In short, southern Florida auto travel requires alertness, concentration, and expecting the unexpected. No doubt, my Snowbird Driving Education has sharpened my road skills.

While we have enjoyed our winter experience in Florida, Kathy and I look forward to returning home. We are rooted in Rhode Island and have missed family and friends that are woven into our life tapestry. We hope to return to south Florida next winter but, "There's no place like home…(with a final caveat)."

Could you arrange for temperature to reach 60 degrees and melt any lingering snow before we pull into our driveway in North Providence?

IMPRESSIONS FROM A 12-DAY HOSPITAL ODYSSEY

Published October 2019, in *PrimeTime magazine.*

The confluence of two bacterial infections and dehydration recently earned me trip to the hospital emergency room. What I thought would be a quick test, diagnosis, and discharge home, armed with assorted medications, became a hospital admission. Thus began a 12-day hospital odyssey, hooked into cocktails of IVs; subjected to a continuous parade of CAT scans, ultrasounds, X-rays; and swallowing a seemingly endless regimen of oral medications. When I was finally discharged, James Taylor's "Isn't it nice to be home again," rang in my ears.

Observations, and the ability to translate those observations into a good yarn, are skills I have acquired after more than 40 years of professional and freelance writing. So it should come as no surprise to you that my hospital stay was the basis for this column.

First and foremost, the compassionate, attentive, and professional care given by nurses and Certified Nursing Assistants must be noted. These dedicated medical staffers were in the front lines of my care and treatment plan every day. They also set a positive tone for my treatment, recovery, and eventual discharge. Their contributions are immeasurable and deserve to be recognized.

Secondly, I believe that hospital beds are designed for people who stand at five feet nothing. The mattresses are narrow, feel like they are stuffed with pebbles, and the mattress covers appear to be made of slip and slide vinyl. No matter how many times you position yourself at the top of the bed, you inevitably creep downward and find your feet dangling over the edge. I have no idea how anybody over five feet would manage comfortably in the standard hospital bed. As you can imagine, sleeping while confined to one of these contraptions is exceedingly difficult. If the administration's goal is to inspire rapid recovery and quick discharge, the hospital bed is a key to achieving these goals.

In addition to impaling different locations on my arms and hands for IV set-ups, I was visited several times each day by the descendents of Count Dracula. Who knew that I had so much blood of interest to so many people?

I will resist the temptation to lower the literary boom on hospital food. After all, I am used to meals featuring homemade gravy (pasta sauce to non-Italians), fresh vegetables, and other culinary delicacies. Considering that the kitchen staff prepares hundreds of meals each day, many with dietary restrictions, the food is generally palatable. The staff is pleasant and I cobbled together a menu of salads, fruit plates, and sandwiches from the daily offerings to keep me nutritionally afloat until my discharge. (Besides, on one of my many walks around the hospital floor I discovered a cache of crackers, peanut butter, graham crackers, and mini-cookies to supplement my caloric intake).

Due my diagnoses, I was visited by a squadron of attending physicians, radiologists, infectious disease (sounds ominous doesn't it?) specialists, and interns every day. While I appreciated their attention and concern for my health, it was difficult to remember who was who and summarize the day's physician visits for my wife. Each doctor was patient in addressing my questions, direct and clear in their assessment of my treatment plan, and they were very involved in planning follow-up visits to assure that my recovery was complete. The coordination between each specialized physician team was very reassuring.

My last observation concerns the hospital staff member that I had instant reservations about-the hospital discharge planner. This basic wariness can be attributed to several unpleasant experiences with hospital discharge planners in my 30-year career in elder services and also serving as a caregiver for an older cousin.

On Day Two of my hospital stay, a "case manager" visited me to discuss my discharge plan. I advised her that my discharge would depend on medical decisions made by my physician teams. Apparently, the message was received loud and clear and our next meeting took place the day before I left the hospital.

I await the inevitable survey soliciting my impressions and input on my 12-day hospital odyssey. It's obvious that the hospital has invested considerable staff training time to assure that patients are treated with courtesy, respect, and dignity. The positive effects of this training are evident from the time I entered the emergency room, to the initial testing and diagnosis, admission, transport, and extending even to hospital maintenance personnel.

Putting aside kibitzing, I admire the professionalism, concern, and compassion of the doctors, nurses, and CNAs. I note the courteous and accommodating service of the dining staff. However, you can be sure that I will offer several pointed remarks about the uncomfortable nature of those short, rocky, slippery hospital beds. Hopefully, my "suggestions" will be used to improve the equipment for future patients.

YES... IT'S HAPPENED AGAIN!

Published May 2020, in *PrimeTime magazine*.

As I predicted in a previous column, it has happened again! The Fates have turned my original plan for this month's column inside out. Observations from my annual pilgrimage to Key West, Florida and its mystical ability to suspend reality will have to wait. The intrusion of the Coronavirus has taken precedence.

As of this writing, the virus is still wreaking havoc on the health, well-being, and economic security of hundreds of thousands of people here in the United State and across the globe. The nightly news and other outlets are laboring diligently to provide medically reliable, scientifically based information to help us deal with this pandemic. A free press has fulfilled its obligation admirably.

Beyond the challenges we face in this humanitarian crisis, there is a unique opportunity. We will have the time to take inventory of those little things we took for granted before the pandemic outbreak. Perhaps after we pause to appreciate these little things, we will never take them for granted again.

Perhaps the most puzzling AND amusing phenomenon is the Great Bathroom Tissue Rush. For many people, this quest has taken on the religious fervor of a search for the Holy Grail. At my own peril and threat to my personal supply of paper goods, I have determined that paper towels, napkins or Kleenex tissues work just as well in an emergency. BUT PLEASE guard this secret closely!

Beyond that, the things that I miss during this new era of "social distancing" are surprisingly simple and mundane. As of early April, Kathy and I remain in Florida. We are disappointed that the beaches of Ft. Lauderdale and small community of Lauderdale-By-The-Sea are officially closed. On a recent drive hugging the shoreline on Ocean Drive (Rte. A1A), we witnessed the eerie site of an empty beach and police cruisers placed at intervals that assured compliance with the "Nobody Allowed on the Beach" edict. Normally busy shops, restaurants, and watering holes on Ocean Drive were shuttered. Normally bustling hotels were virtually devoid of guests. And the empty parking lots resembled asphalt and concrete wastelands. With only negligible foot traffic on the beachfront walkway, Ft. Lauderdale had taken on appearance of a South Florida ghost town.

I miss our Sunday morning routine of attending Mass at the local Catholic Church and going out for breakfast afterwards. Somehow, online and Facebook broadcasts of Mass is a less than-desirable substitute for in-person weekly prayer and reflection.

Our freedom to travel has been suspended. The date for our return drive home to North Providence is uncertain due to restrictions on hotels and restaurants. The patchwork pattern of "sheltering in place" directives up and down the East Coast is responsible for the delay. (In an interesting case of role reversal, we are continuingly admonished by our children, via e-mail and telephone lectures, to stay in Florida for a while longer).

I miss weekly golf outings and dinner with my friends after the round. I miss the (infrequent) "high-fives" after I've made a great shot and the traditional handshakes after a match.

I missed the bracket busting upsets in college basketball's yearly imitation of a Roman chariot race in the Coliseum-March Madness. It's the only athletic extravaganza where college-basketball neophytes could win the office pool by selecting winners by uniform color, nickname, and any other uniquely personal and baffling system.

The simple act of grocery shopping has taken on the uncertainty of a Lewis and Clark expedition. You never know what you are going (or not) to find. The pandemic has renewed my admiration and appreciation for medical personnel, law enforcement officials, first responders, grocery store staff, pharmacists, and other workers dealing with the public every day to supply us with the basic needs of life, and who labor every day to safeguard our health, well-being, and safety.

Mostly, I miss hugging, kissing, and talking with my children Kate, Matt, and Ben. Matt lives in Las Vegas and Ben lives in New Jersey. While we talk often, somehow the distance between us seems wider during this forced social isolation. Kate lives in North Providence and is the mother of our 16-year-old twin granddaughters Kailyn and

Sophia, and 10-year-old grandson Nicholas. Currently we are limited to phone calls and e-mail messages. The high school softball season for Kailyn and Sophia and Nick's newest sporting venture, lacrosse, will have to wait, if they happen at all. Perhaps more importantly to the twins, the road test, the final hurdle in their quest for the coveted driver's license has been delayed. Our one -year old grandson Benjamin, Junior has a limited vocabulary so we enjoy each other's company via FaceTime and virtual hugs.

The Coronavirus pandemic had brought our lives to a halt and altered our every day experiences. It's strange to wake up in the morning and realize that life, as we know it, has been temporarily suspended in time and space. At the same time, the pandemic has provided an opportunity to pause, be thankful for the gifts we have, and appreciate those moments we spend with our family and friends. Take advantage of that opportunity.

(ALMOST)
EPILOGUE

"I don't like the word 'autobiography." I rather like the term 'auto-fiction.' The second you make a script out of the story of your life, it becomes fictional. Of course, the truth is never far. But the story is created out of it."

–Marjane Satarpi

Shortly after reviewing the first draft of *Fifty Shades of Life, Love, and Laughter* I realized that I had written much of the script for my life journey. Without knowing it, I had written my "auto-fiction" (I guess, according to above reference) in stories of 1,000 words or less! In many ways, I had come a long way from my Crary roots, but I have not abandoned my history, nor forgotten the people were part of my life experiences.

Fifty Shades of Life, Love, and Laughter has renewed my appreciation and wonder of the joys, contradictions, and absurdities of life; deepened my gratitude for the unconditional love and encouragement of my family and friends; and made me laugh (mostly at myself) at the idiosyncrasies, ironies, and comic (and cosmic) forces I encounter every day. For these gifts, and many other recollections of long ago that mysteriously and suddenly re-appear in the lenses of my memory, I am thankful.

Maybe the next Fifty Shades are awaiting my discovery.

Made in United States
North Haven, CT
25 June 2023

38226398R00105